Photo of Me

1999

This Millennium Yearbook belongs to

_____

_____

TIMELINE

Millennium Yearbook

2000

My Personal Record

WOLFHOUND PRESS
Celebrating 25 *Years*

Published 1999 by
Wolfhound Press Ltd
68 Mountjoy Square
Dublin 1

The Arts Council
An Chomhairle Ealaíon

Wolfhound Press receives financial assistance from the Arts Council/An Chomhairle Ealaíon, Dublin

Every effort has been made to ensure the accuracy of facts and figures contained in this book. The publishers accept no responsibility for inadvertent errors.

British Library Cataloguing-in-Publication Data
A catalogue record for this book is available from the British Library

ISBN 0-86327-749-7

Cover design: Azure
Typesetting: Wolfhound Press
Layout: Wolfhound Press and Soracha Cashman
Printed in the Republic of Ireland by Colour Books Limited, Dublin

Introduction to a New Millennium...

Between the covers of this book is your personal millennium time capsule.

For each day, there's a space in which you can keep track of your appointments or write down what you did on that day. For each week, there's also a space for World Events, where you can keep a record of the biggest news events of that week; a 'My World' space, where you can write down the most important events in your own life; and a Fact File, which will tell you some of the things that happened in that week over the past millennium. There are also spaces where you can write about your family and friends, describe your life — your school, your clothes, your favourite TV programmes — glue in photographs of yourself, your holidays, your favourite actors and singers — and much more!

This yearbook tells the month-by-month stories of Art, a boy living at the beginning of the first millennium, and Finn and Ita, twins living at the beginning of the second millennium. By the end of the year, it will also tell the story of someone living at the beginning of the third millennium — you.

This yearbook will help you capture the year 2000 forever. Go back and re-read it in ten, twenty or fifty years — and remember what the beginning of the new millennium was like for you.

ABOUT ART

Roman ships actually did visit Ireland at the beginning of the first millennium. At that time, most people didn't know how to write, but the druids did use two different forms of writing. One form used Roman letters, although the words were in the Celtic language. The other form was Ogham, a secret code where each letter is made up of knife-strokes written above, below, or through a line, or sometimes to the sides of the line.

About Finn and Ita

Although Finn and Ita's story takes place a thousand years after Art's, their home is in the same place as his: by the black pool which gave Dublin its name, near where Dublin Castle stands today. In Finn and Ita's time, around the year 1000, Dublin was a busy Viking settlement. Recently, when Fishamble Street (near Christchurch) was excavated, archaeologists discovered the remains of Viking shops and workplaces — shoemakers', comb-makers', weavers', potters', bronzesmiths', blacksmiths' — and pieces of the boats they made.

December **December** **December** **December** **December**

25 Saturday

26 Sunday

* World Events

! My World

? Fact File

Christmas
Day

2000 2000 2000 2000 2000 2000 2000 2000 2000 2000 2000 2000 2000

St Stephen's
Day

2000 2000 2000 2000 2000 2000 2000 2000 2000 2000 2000 2000 2000

2000 2000 2000 2000 2000 2000 2000 2000 2000 2000 2000 2000 2000

2000 2000 2000 2000 2000 2000 2000 2000 2000 2000 2000 2000 2000

2000 2000 2000 2000 2000 2000 2000 2000 2000 2000 2000 2000 2000

On 26 December 1591 Red Hugh O'Donnell and Henry Art O'Neill escaped from Dublin Castle, where they were being held prisoner, and fled to the Dublin mountains. O'Neill died there of exposure, but O'Donnell managed to get back to his home in Donegal.

December

27 Monday
2000 2000 2000 2000 2000 2000 2000 2000 2000 2000 2000 2000 2000

Holiday
UK and Rep.
of Ireland

28 Tuesday
2000 2000 2000 2000 2000 2000 2000 2000 2000 2000 2000 2000 2000

Holiday
UK and Rep.
of Ireland

29 Wednesday
2000 2000 2000 2000 2000 2000 2000 2000 2000 2000 2000 2000 2000

Last Quarter

30 Thursday
2000 2000 2000 2000 2000 2000 2000 2000 2000 2000 2000 2000 2000

31 Friday
2000 2000 2000 2000 2000 2000 2000 2000 2000 2000 2000 2000 2000

New Year's
Eve

My favourite memories of New Year's Eve 1999

My New Year's resolutions for the year 2000

(If you want to keep your resolutions extra-secret, why not tape a photo over them like a flap?)

On this page, glue in your favourite picture from the twentieth century. This could be anything from a holiday snap to a newspaper clipping, from a moon-landing image to a picture of JFK.

It's up to you — what's your favourite image from this century?

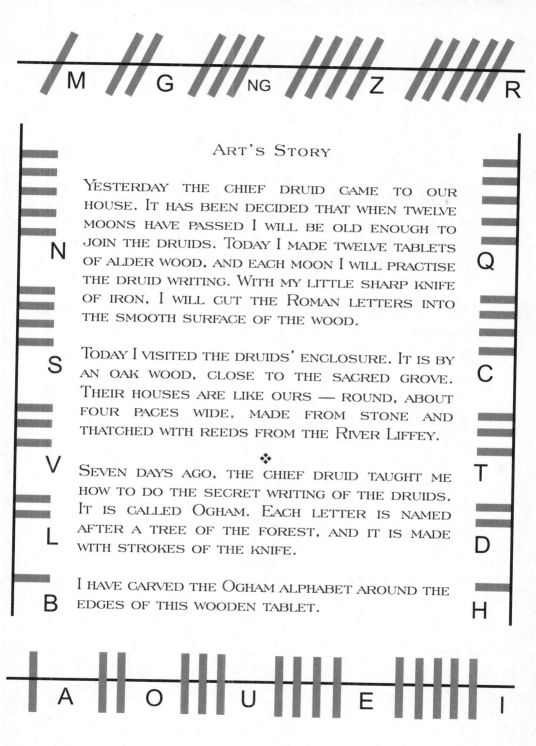

Art's Story

Yesterday the chief druid came to our house. It has been decided that when twelve moons have passed I will be old enough to join the druids. Today I made twelve tablets of alder wood, and each moon I will practise the druid writing. With my little sharp knife of iron, I will cut the Roman letters into the smooth surface of the wood.

Today I visited the druids' enclosure. It is by an oak wood, close to the sacred grove. Their houses are like ours — round, about four paces wide, made from stone and thatched with reeds from the River Liffey.

❖

Seven days ago, the chief druid taught me how to do the secret writing of the druids. It is called Ogham. Each letter is named after a tree of the forest, and it is made with strokes of the knife.

I have carved the Ogham alphabet around the edges of this wooden tablet.

Finn's Story

To mark the beginning of the new millennium, the monks have given me and my twin sister, Ita, a gift: twelve small pieces of parchment, some fine goose-feathers, and a pot of ink made from soot mixed with honey.

'Each month you must write down all that happens to you in this important year,' said one monk. 'Finn must write the first month, Ita the second, and so on.'

The first thing to write is the saddest thing that has happened to us in all our twelve summers: our father can't work any more. He used to make boats on the black pool called Dublin, and sell them to traders and people who were going adventuring, but now no one will buy his boats.

He sits at home and Mother cries.

01 Saturday

02 Sunday

* World Events

! My World

? Fact File

New Year's Day

Holiday UK and Rep. of Ireland

2000 2000 2000 2000 2000 2000 2000 2000 2000 2000 2000 2000 2000

2000 2000 2000 2000 2000 2000 2000 2000 2000 2000 2000 2000 2000

2000 2000 2000 2000 2000 2000 2000 2000 2000 2000 2000 2000 2000

2000 2000 2000 2000 2000 2000 2000 2000 2000 2000 2000 2000 2000

2000 2000 2000 2000 2000 2000 2000 2000 2000 2000 2000 2000 2000

On 1 January 1801 the Act of Union became law. This meant that Ireland and Britain were united under the same parliament.

January **03** Monday

2000 2000 2000 2000 2000 2000 2000 2000 2000 2000 2000 2000 2000

Holiday
UK and Rep.
of Ireland

January **04** Tuesday

2000 2000 2000 2000 2000 2000 2000 2000 2000 2000 2000 2000 2000

Holiday
Scotland

January **05** Wednesday

2000 2000 2000 2000 2000 2000 2000 2000 2000 2000 2000 2000 2000

January **06** Thursday

2000 2000 2000 2000 2000 2000 2000 2000 2000 2000 2000 2000 2000

New Moon

Epiphany

January **07** Friday

2000 2000 2000 2000 2000 2000 2000 2000 2000 2000 2000 2000 2000

08

January

Saturday

09

Sunday

*

World
Events

!

My World

?

Fact File

January

January

January

2000 2000 2000 2000 2000 2000 2000 2000 2000 2000 2000 2000 2000

2000 2000 2000 2000 2000 2000 2000 2000 2000 2000 2000 2000 2000

2000 2000 2000 2000 2000 2000 2000 2000 2000 2000 2000 2000 2000

2000 2000 2000 2000 2000 2000 2000 2000 2000 2000 2000 2000 2000

2000 2000 2000 2000 2000 2000 2000 2000 2000 2000 2000 2000 2000

On 9 January 1594 Trinity College Dublin opened to students. Trinity was Ireland's first university. It had been founded by Queen Elizabeth in 1592. None of the original Elizabethan buildings are still standing.

January **10** Monday

2000 2000 2000 2000 2000 2000 2000 2000 2000 2000 2000 2000 2000

January **11** Tuesday

2000 2000 2000 2000 2000 2000 2000 2000 2000 2000 2000 2000 2000

January **12** Wednesday

2000 2000 2000 2000 2000 2000 2000 2000 2000 2000 2000 2000 2000

January **13** Thursday

2000 2000 2000 2000 2000 2000 2000 2000 2000 2000 2000 2000 2000

January **14** Friday

2000 2000 2000 2000 2000 2000 2000 2000 2000 2000 2000 2000 2000

First
Quarter

2000 2000 2000 2000 2000 2000 2000 2000 2000 2000 2000 2000 2000

2000 2000 2000 2000 2000 2000 2000 2000 2000 2000 2000 2000 2000

2000 2000 2000 2000 2000 2000 2000 2000 2000 2000 2000 2000 2000

2000 2000 2000 2000 2000 2000 2000 2000 2000 2000 2000 2000 2000

2000 2000 2000 2000 2000 2000 2000 2000 2000 2000 2000 2000 2000

On 13 January 1941 James Joyce died. He is especially famous for his novel *Ulysses*, which is set in Dublin on 16 June. The main character is called Leopold Bloom, and 16 June is now celebrated in Dublin as Bloomsday.

15 Saturday

16 Sunday

* World Events

! My World

? Fact File

January January January

17

Monday

2000 2000 2000 2000 2000 2000 2000 2000 2000 2000 2000 2000 2000

18

Tuesday

2000 2000 2000 2000 2000 2000 2000 2000 2000 2000 2000 2000 2000

19

Wednesday

2000 2000 2000 2000 2000 2000 2000 2000 2000 2000 2000 2000 2000

20

Thursday

2000 2000 2000 2000 2000 2000 2000 2000 2000 2000 2000 2000 2000

Aquarius
20 January -
18 February

21

Friday

2000 2000 2000 2000 2000 2000 2000 2000 2000 2000 2000 2000 2000

Full Moon

Total Eclipse
of the Moon

2000 2000 2000 2000 2000 2000 2000 2000 2000 2000 2000 2000 2000

2000 2000 2000 2000 2000 2000 2000 2000 2000 2000 2000 2000 2000

2000 2000 2000 2000 2000 2000 2000 2000 2000 2000 2000 2000 2000

2000 2000 2000 2000 2000 2000 2000 2000 2000 2000 2000 2000 2000

2000 2000 2000 2000 2000 2000 2000 2000 2000 2000 2000 2000 2000

On 19 January 1785 Richard Crosbie became Ireland's first airman. He went up in a hot-air balloon from Ranelagh in Dublin.

24
Monday

2000 2000 2000 2000 2000 2000 2000 2000 2000 2000 2000 2000 2000

25
Tuesday

2000 2000 2000 2000 2000 2000 2000 2000 2000 2000 2000 2000 2000

26
Wednesday

2000 2000 2000 2000 2000 2000 2000 2000 2000 2000 2000 2000 2000

27
Thursday

2000 2000 2000 2000 2000 2000 2000 2000 2000 2000 2000 2000 2000

28
Friday

2000 2000 2000 2000 2000 2000 2000 2000 2000 2000 2000 2000 2000

Last Quarter

2000 2000 2000 2000 2000 2000 2000 2000 2000 2000 2000 2000 2000

2000 2000 2000 2000 2000 2000 2000 2000 2000 2000 2000 2000 2000

2000 2000 2000 2000 2000 2000 2000 2000 2000 2000 2000 2000 2000

2000 2000 2000 2000 2000 2000 2000 2000 2000 2000 2000 2000 2000

2000 2000 2000 2000 2000 2000 2000 2000 2000 2000 2000 2000 2000

On 30 January 1864 the National Gallery of Ireland was opened. It is still located in the original building on Merrion Square in Dublin, but several extensions have been added to it over the years.

January

29 Saturday

30 Sunday

January

* World Events

! My World

? Fact File

January

January

*

World Events

! My World

? Fact File

2000 2000 2000 2000 2000 2000 2000 2000 2000 2000 2000 2000 2000

Our World
The areas of our greatest oceans are:

Pacific: 165,767,000 sq. km   Atlantic: 82,238,000 sq. km

Indian: 73,446,000 sq. km   Arctic: 14,059,000 sq. km

2000 2000 2000 2000 2000 2000 2000 2000 2000 2000 2000 2000 2000

2000 2000 2000 2000 2000 2000 2000 2000 2000 2000 2000 2000 2000

2000 2000 2000 2000 2000 2000 2000 2000 2000 2000 2000 2000 2000

On 31 January 1913 the Ulster Volunteer Force was founded in Belfast by General Sir George Richardson and Captain Wilfred Spender. The purpose of the Force was to fight to keep Ulster a part of the United Kingdom.

MY FAMILY

There are ____ people in my family. Their names are:

My family pet is called _____

Our car is a _____

Below is a picture of my family.

_____
_____
_____
_____
_____
_____

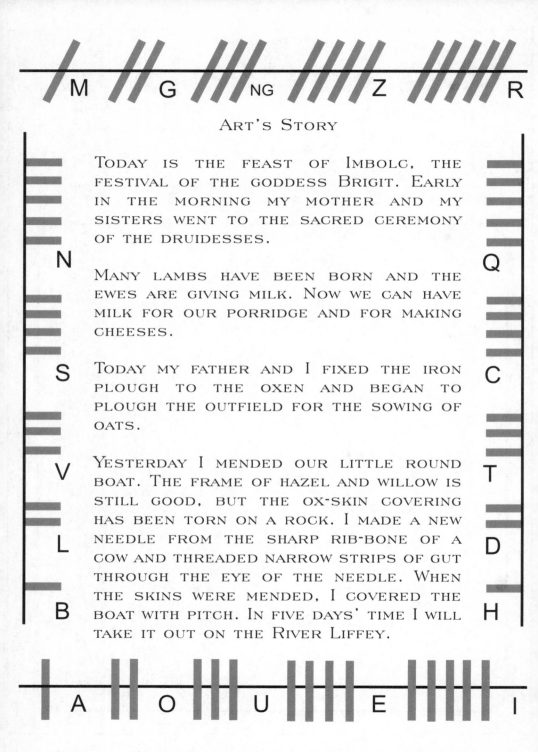

Art's Story

Today is the feast of Imbolc, the festival of the goddess Brigit. Early in the morning my mother and my sisters went to the sacred ceremony of the druidesses.

Many lambs have been born and the ewes are giving milk. Now we can have milk for our porridge and for making cheeses.

Today my father and I fixed the iron plough to the oxen and began to plough the outfield for the sowing of oats.

Yesterday I mended our little round boat. The frame of hazel and willow is still good, but the ox-skin covering has been torn on a rock. I made a new needle from the sharp rib-bone of a cow and threaded narrow strips of gut through the eye of the needle. When the skins were mended, I covered the boat with pitch. In five days' time I will take it out on the River Liffey.

Ita's Story

When Finn wrote those words, it was the time of the new moon. The moon waxed and waned, and then another new moon came, but our Viking father still hasn't been able to work building his boats. (Like Sitric Silkbeard, King of Dublin, Finn and I have a Viking father and an Irish mother.) We used to watch him making the boats, sawing, shaving, hammering.... But then it happened. Angry voices, complaints, quarrels — Father's boats had begun to sink. They would float well for an hour or so, but then water would seep in. Cargo was lost and men were drowned.

'Some evil god has done this to me,' cried Father. But we're Christians and we don't believe in evil gods.

'Some evil man,' Finn said to me privately, and I agree with him.

February

February February February February February

2000 2000 2000 2000 2000 2000 2000 2000 2000 2000 2000 2000 2000

Our World
The surface areas of our largest deserts are:

Sahara: 9,067,000 sq. km   Arabian: 2,330,000 sq. km
Australian: 1,550,000 sq. km   Gobi: 1,166,000 sq. km

01 Tuesday

2000 2000 2000 2000 2000 2000 2000 2000 2000 2000 2000 2000 2000

02 Wednesday

2000 2000 2000 2000 2000 2000 2000 2000 2000 2000 2000 2000 2000

03 Thursday

2000 2000 2000 2000 2000 2000 2000 2000 2000 2000 2000 2000 2000

04 Friday

2000 2000 2000 2000 2000 2000 2000 2000 2000 2000 2000 2000 2000

05 February

Saturday

06 February

Sunday

* World Events

! My World

? Fact File

New Moon

Yuan Tan
(Chinese
New Year)

2000 2000 2000 2000 2000 2000 2000 2000 2000 2000 2000 2000 2000

2000 2000 2000 2000 2000 2000 2000 2000 2000 2000 2000 2000 2000

2000 2000 2000 2000 2000 2000 2000 2000 2000 2000 2000 2000 2000

2000 2000 2000 2000 2000 2000 2000 2000 2000 2000 2000 2000 2000

2000 2000 2000 2000 2000 2000 2000 2000 2000 2000 2000 2000 2000

On 1 February 1982 it became illegal in Ireland for teachers to slap or hit schoolchildren. Before that, it was common for the cane to be used to punish pupils who were bold or who didn't know their lessons.

February

February

February

February

07 Monday

08 Tuesday

09 Wednesday

10 Thursday

11 Friday

2000 2000 2000 2000 2000 2000 2000 2000 2000 2000 2000 2000 2000

2000 2000 2000 2000 2000 2000 2000 2000 2000 2000 2000 2000 2000

2000 2000 2000 2000 2000 2000 2000 2000 2000 2000 2000 2000 2000

2000 2000 2000 2000 2000 2000 2000 2000 2000 2000 2000 2000 2000

2000 2000 2000 2000 2000 2000 2000 2000 2000 2000 2000 2000 2000

First Quarter

2000 2000 2000 2000 2000 2000 2000 2000 2000 2000 2000 2000 2000

2000 2000 2000 2000 2000 2000 2000 2000 2000 2000 2000 2000 2000

2000 2000 2000 2000 2000 2000 2000 2000 2000 2000 2000 2000 2000

2000 2000 2000 2000 2000 2000 2000 2000 2000 2000 2000 2000 2000

2000 2000 2000 2000 2000 2000 2000 2000 2000 2000 2000 2000 2000

On 9 February 1923 Brendan Behan was born. He became a famous Irish writer and a well-known character around Dublin. His autobiography, *Borstal Boy*, describes the time he spent in reform school in Britain.

12 February
Saturday

13 February
Sunday

* February
World Events

! February
My World

? February
Fact File

February

14 Monday
2000 2000 2000 2000 2000 2000 2000 2000 2000 2000 2000 2000 2000

St Valentine's Day

15 Tuesday
2000 2000 2000 2000 2000 2000 2000 2000 2000 2000 2000 2000 2000

16 Wednesday
2000 2000 2000 2000 2000 2000 2000 2000 2000 2000 2000 2000 2000

17 Thursday
2000 2000 2000 2000 2000 2000 2000 2000 2000 2000 2000 2000 2000

18 Friday
2000 2000 2000 2000 2000 2000 2000 2000 2000 2000 2000 2000 2000

February 19 Saturday

February 20 Sunday

* World Events

! My World

? Fact File

February February February February

Full Moon

Pisces
19 February -
20 March

2000 2000 2000 2000 2000 2000 2000 2000 2000 2000 2000 2000 2000

2000 2000 2000 2000 2000 2000 2000 2000 2000 2000 2000 2000 2000

2000 2000 2000 2000 2000 2000 2000 2000 2000 2000 2000 2000 2000

2000 2000 2000 2000 2000 2000 2000 2000 2000 2000 2000 2000 2000

2000 2000 2000 2000 2000 2000 2000 2000 2000 2000 2000 2000 2000

On 18 February 1366 the Statutes of Kilkenny were
passed. These laws meant that Norman-Irish people
weren't allowed to speak Irish or to marry Irish people.

February

February

21 Monday

2000 2000 2000 2000 2000 2000 2000 2000 2000 2000 2000 2000 2000

22 Tuesday

2000 2000 2000 2000 2000 2000 2000 2000 2000 2000 2000 2000 2000

23 Wednesday

2000 2000 2000 2000 2000 2000 2000 2000 2000 2000 2000 2000 2000

24 Thursday

2000 2000 2000 2000 2000 2000 2000 2000 2000 2000 2000 2000 2000

25 Friday

2000 2000 2000 2000 2000 2000 2000 2000 2000 2000 2000 2000 2000

26
February
Saturday

27
February
Sunday

* World Events
February

! My World
February

? Fact File
February

Last Quarter

2000 2000 2000 2000 2000 2000 2000 2000 2000 2000 2000 2000 2000

2000 2000 2000 2000 2000 2000 2000 2000 2000 2000 2000 2000 2000

2000 2000 2000 2000 2000 2000 2000 2000 2000 2000 2000 2000 2000

2000 2000 2000 2000 2000 2000 2000 2000 2000 2000 2000 2000 2000

2000 2000 2000 2000 2000 2000 2000 2000 2000 2000 2000 2000 2000

On 26 February 1914 the *Britannic*, the sister ship of the *Titanic*, was launched in Belfast.

28 Monday

29 Tuesday

* World Events

! My World

? Fact File

2000 2000 2000 2000 2000 2000 2000 2000 2000 2000 2000 2000 2000

2000 2000 2000 2000 2000 2000 2000 2000 2000 2000 2000 2000 2000

2000 2000 2000 2000 2000 2000 2000 2000 2000 2000 2000 2000 2000

2000 2000 2000 2000 2000 2000 2000 2000 2000 2000 2000 2000 2000

2000 2000 2000 2000 2000 2000 2000 2000 2000 2000 2000 2000 2000

On 28 February 1743 James Gandon was born. He became an architect and designed the Four Courts in Dublin. They were completed in 1801 and destroyed in 1922, during the Civil War. They were rebuilt and are still in use.

THE FUTURE

What do you think the new millennium holds for you? Write down your top ten wishes, or describe what you think your life will be like in ten, twenty or fifty years. Someday in the future, when you re-read this yearbook, you'll find out whether you were right!

Art's Story

The sun has risen and set many times since I last wrote. When I took the boat out on the river, I went too far and was carried down to the sea. A Roman ship was there, a tall ship with a sail and six banks of oarsmen. A man threw a net at my little boat and caught me like a fish. Now I am a slave of that man.

I begin to understand the Roman tongue — Latin, it is called. These Romans are not going back to their own country, but to a country called Gaul, which they have captured. They tell me that one day they will come and capture Ireland, but now they are just finding out about it — what will grow there and what its riches are.

❖

Today we saw the coast of Gaul. Tomorrow we will land.

Finn's Story

Another new moon has come, and Ita and I are in despair. We have very little food, and we can't study with the monks any more, because we don't have a silver penny to pay them with.

'Let's talk to the monks, anyway,' said Ita. 'They can say prayers to cast out the devil, even if Father believes it's an evil god.'

⌘

The monks came and said their prayers, and it worked. Father is cheerful again. He has borrowed some money from his brothers and started work on a new boat.

⌘

The keel of the boat has been built, from the trunk of an oak tree the length of two men. Father has spent a lot of time shaping its sharp edge so that it will cut through the water more speedily than any other boat on the River Liffey.

2000 2000 2000 2000 2000 2000 2000 2000 2000 2000 2000 2000 2000

Our World
The heights in metres of our highest mountains are:

Everest:	8,848m	K2:	8,611m
Kanchenjunga:	8,586m	Lhotse:	8,511m
Makalu 1:	8,481m	Dhaulagiri 1:	8,172m
Manaslu:	8,156m	Cho Oyu:	8,153m
Nanga Parbat:	8,125m	Annapurna:	8,091m

01 Wednesday

2000 2000 2000 2000 2000 2000 2000 2000 2000 2000 2000 2000 2000

02 Thursday

2000 2000 2000 2000 2000 2000 2000 2000 2000 2000 2000 2000 2000

03 Friday

2000 2000 2000 2000 2000 2000 2000 2000 2000 2000 2000 2000 2000

04
Saturday

05
Sunday

* World Events

! My World

? Fact File

March March March March March

2000 2000 2000 2000 2000 2000 2000 2000 2000 2000 2000 2000 2000

2000 2000 2000 2000 2000 2000 2000 2000 2000 2000 2000 2000 2000

2000 2000 2000 2000 2000 2000 2000 2000 2000 2000 2000 2000 2000

2000 2000 2000 2000 2000 2000 2000 2000 2000 2000 2000 2000 2000

2000 2000 2000 2000 2000 2000 2000 2000 2000 2000 2000 2000 2000

On 5 March 1867 a Fenian rising took place in Counties Dublin, Wicklow, Tipperary, Limerick, Clare, Louth and Cork. It was a complete failure.

March

06 Monday
2000 2000 2000 2000 2000 2000 2000 2000 2000 2000 2000 2000 2000

New Moon

07 Tuesday
2000 2000 2000 2000 2000 2000 2000 2000 2000 2000 2000 2000 2000

Shrove
Tuesday

08 Wednesday
2000 2000 2000 2000 2000 2000 2000 2000 2000 2000 2000 2000 2000

Ash
Wednesday

09 Thursday
2000 2000 2000 2000 2000 2000 2000 2000 2000 2000 2000 2000 2000

10 Friday
2000 2000 2000 2000 2000 2000 2000 2000 2000 2000 2000 2000 2000

11 March Saturday

12 March Sunday

* World Events

! My World

? Fact File

March

2000 2000 2000 2000 2000 2000 2000 2000 2000 2000 2000 2000 2000

2000 2000 2000 2000 2000 2000 2000 2000 2000 2000 2000 2000 2000

2000 2000 2000 2000 2000 2000 2000 2000 2000 2000 2000 2000 2000

2000 2000 2000 2000 2000 2000 2000 2000 2000 2000 2000 2000 2000

2000 2000 2000 2000 2000 2000 2000 2000 2000 2000 2000 2000 2000

On 11 March 1596 a cargo of barrels of gunpowder exploded at Winetavern Street in Dublin. A spark from a horseshoe caused the explosion, in which 120 people were killed.

13

Monday

2000 2000 2000 2000 2000 2000 2000 2000 2000 2000 2000 2000 2000

First Quarter

14

Tuesday

2000 2000 2000 2000 2000 2000 2000 2000 2000 2000 2000 2000 2000

15

Wednesday

2000 2000 2000 2000 2000 2000 2000 2000 2000 2000 2000 2000 2000

16

Thursday

2000 2000 2000 2000 2000 2000 2000 2000 2000 2000 2000 2000 2000

17

Friday

2000 2000 2000 2000 2000 2000 2000 2000 2000 2000 2000 2000 2000

St Patrick's Day

Holiday Rep. of Ireland and N. Ireland

2000 2000 2000 2000 2000 2000 2000 2000 2000 2000 2000 2000 2000

2000 2000 2000 2000 2000 2000 2000 2000 2000 2000 2000 2000 2000

2000 2000 2000 2000 2000 2000 2000 2000 2000 2000 2000 2000 2000

2000 2000 2000 2000 2000 2000 2000 2000 2000 2000 2000 2000 2000

2000 2000 2000 2000 2000 2000 2000 2000 2000 2000 2000 2000 2000

On 15 March 1852 Lady Augusta Gregory was born. She was a playwright and one of the founders of Dublin's Abbey Theatre, which opened in 1904 (on the site of the city morgue!)

18 Saturday — March

19 Sunday — March

* World Events — March

! My World

? Fact File — March

March

20 Monday

2000 2000 2000 2000 2000 2000 2000 2000 2000 2000 2000 2000 2000

Full Moon

21 Tuesday

2000 2000 2000 2000 2000 2000 2000 2000 2000 2000 2000 2000 2000

Aries
21 March -
19 April

22 Wednesday

2000 2000 2000 2000 2000 2000 2000 2000 2000 2000 2000 2000 2000

23 Thursday

2000 2000 2000 2000 2000 2000 2000 2000 2000 2000 2000 2000 2000

24 Friday

2000 2000 2000 2000 2000 2000 2000 2000 2000 2000 2000 2000 2000

2000 2000 2000 2000 2000 2000 2000 2000 2000 2000 2000 2000 2000

2000 2000 2000 2000 2000 2000 2000 2000 2000 2000 2000 2000 2000

2000 2000 2000 2000 2000 2000 2000 2000 2000 2000 2000 2000 2000

2000 2000 2000 2000 2000 2000 2000 2000 2000 2000 2000 2000 2000

2000 2000 2000 2000 2000 2000 2000 2000 2000 2000 2000 2000 2000

On 25 March 1920 the 'Black and Tans' arrived in Ireland. They were ex-soldiers from the British Army, who were sent to Ireland to help the Irish police during the War of Independence.

25
Saturday

March

26
Sunday

March

*
World
Events

!
My World

March

?
Fact File

March

March

27 Monday

2000 2000 2000 2000 2000 2000 2000 2000 2000 2000 2000 2000 2000

March

28 Tuesday

2000 2000 2000 2000 2000 2000 2000 2000 2000 2000 2000 2000 2000

Last Quarter

March

29 Wednesday

2000 2000 2000 2000 2000 2000 2000 2000 2000 2000 2000 2000 2000

March

30 Thursday

2000 2000 2000 2000 2000 2000 2000 2000 2000 2000 2000 2000 2000

March

31 Friday

2000 2000 2000 2000 2000 2000 2000 2000 2000 2000 2000 2000 2000

Our World

The cities with the largest populations are:

Toyko, Japan:	26,800,000	São Paolo, Brazil:	16,400,000
New York, USA:	16,300,000	Mexico City, Mexico:	15,600,000
Bombay, India:	15,200,000	Shanghai, China:	15,100,000
Los Angeles, USA:	12,500,000	Beijing, China:	12,400,000
Calcutta, India:	11,700,000	Seoul, South Korea:	11,600,000

On 30 March 1880 Sean O'Casey was born in Dublin. He became a famous playwright. His plays about Dublin include *The Plough and the Stars*, *The Shadow of a Gunman*, and *Juno and the Paycock*.

March

March

March

March

World Events

My World

Fact File

MUSIC

My favourite band is called _____

The lead singer is called _____

My favourite album is called _____

My favourite song is called _____

My favourite music video is called _____

This is a picture of my favourite singer/musician

Art's Story

I am living in a Roman camp in Gaul. There are other slaves here, too. We live in leather tents set out, like trees in a forest, along the sides of streets which cross the camp like plough-furrows. There are other slaves here, also. Tomorrow we will be making a road.

The centurion has measured out a thousand paces. This is called a 'mile', the Latin word meaning 'thousand'. The band of one hundred men that my master belongs to will build this section of the new road.

❖

We have spent the last three days digging out a bed for the new road. Today we began to fill the bed with small stones called gravel.

Next we will put larger stones on top of the gravel. The road will be made higher in the centre, so that the rainwater will run off the road and down drains at the sides.

Ita's Story

Father has begun nailing the strakes, or planks, to the curved prow. The boat has begun to take shape. Everyone living in our street comes to look at it.

⌘

Yesterday Finn and I helped Father to make the holes in the side of the boat so that the oars can be slotted in. We rubbed the oars with the spokeshave until they were as smooth as silk.

Today, Ivar the shoemaker came to look at the boat. He said he wanted to buy it, but Finn and I don't believe him. We think he just came because he's curious. Why should he buy a boat from Father? His daughter married a boat-builder last year. Surely, if he wants a boat to carry his shoes to other markets, he'll buy one from his daughter's husband.

April Fool's
Day

2000 2000 2000 2000 2000 2000 2000 2000 2000 2000 2000 2000 2000

Mother's Day

2000 2000 2000 2000 2000 2000 2000 2000 2000 2000 2000 2000 2000

2000 2000 2000 2000 2000 2000 2000 2000 2000 2000 2000 2000 2000

2000 2000 2000 2000 2000 2000 2000 2000 2000 2000 2000 2000 2000

2000 2000 2000 2000 2000 2000 2000 2000 2000 2000 2000 2000 2000

On 2 April 1972 Raidió na Gaeltachta was launched. It was over twenty years before a national Irish-language television station was started.

01 Saturday
April

02 Sunday
April

* World Events

! My World
April

? Fact File
April

03

Monday

2000 2000 2000 2000 2000 2000 2000 2000 2000 2000 2000 2000 2000

04

Tuesday

2000 2000 2000 2000 2000 2000 2000 2000 2000 2000 2000 2000 2000

New Moon

05

Wednesday

2000 2000 2000 2000 2000 2000 2000 2000 2000 2000 2000 2000 2000

06

Thursday

2000 2000 2000 2000 2000 2000 2000 2000 2000 2000 2000 2000 2000

07

Friday

2000 2000 2000 2000 2000 2000 2000 2000 2000 2000 2000 2000 2000

08

Saturday

April

09

Sunday

April

*

World
Events

April

!

My World

?

Fact File

April

2000 2000 2000 2000 2000 2000 2000 2000 2000 2000 2000 2000 2000

2000 2000 2000 2000 2000 2000 2000 2000 2000 2000 2000 2000 2000

2000 2000 2000 2000 2000 2000 2000 2000 2000 2000 2000 2000 2000

2000 2000 2000 2000 2000 2000 2000 2000 2000 2000 2000 2000 2000

2000 2000 2000 2000 2000 2000 2000 2000 2000 2000 2000 2000 2000

On 5 April 1855 the Dublin-to-Belfast railway line was completed. During parts of the IRA's campaign, particularly in the 1980s, the line became a target for bombs.

April

10 Monday

2000 2000 2000 2000 2000 2000 2000 2000 2000 2000 2000 2000 2000

11 Tuesday

2000 2000 2000 2000 2000 2000 2000 2000 2000 2000 2000 2000 2000

First Quarter

12 Wednesday

2000 2000 2000 2000 2000 2000 2000 2000 2000 2000 2000 2000 2000

13 Thursday

2000 2000 2000 2000 2000 2000 2000 2000 2000 2000 2000 2000 2000

14 Friday

2000 2000 2000 2000 2000 2000 2000 2000 2000 2000 2000 2000 2000

2000 2000 2000 2000 2000 2000 2000 2000 2000 2000 2000 2000 2000

Palm Sunday

2000 2000 2000 2000 2000 2000 2000 2000 2000 2000 2000 2000 2000

2000 2000 2000 2000 2000 2000 2000 2000 2000 2000 2000 2000 2000

2000 2000 2000 2000 2000 2000 2000 2000 2000 2000 2000 2000 2000

2000 2000 2000 2000 2000 2000 2000 2000 2000 2000 2000 2000 2000

On 15 April 1912 the *Titanic* sank when it hit an iceberg off Newfoundland, killing over 1,500 people. The ship was built in the Harland & Wolff shipyard in Belfast.

15 Saturday

16 Sunday

April

*
World Events

April

!
My World

?
Fact File

April

April

17 Monday

2000 2000 2000 2000 2000 2000 2000 2000 2000 2000 2000 2000 2000

18 Tuesday

2000 2000 2000 2000 2000 2000 2000 2000 2000 2000 2000 2000 2000

Full Moon

19 Wednesday

2000 2000 2000 2000 2000 2000 2000 2000 2000 2000 2000 2000 2000

20 Thursday

2000 2000 2000 2000 2000 2000 2000 2000 2000 2000 2000 2000 2000

Taurus
20 April -
20 May

Pesach begins

21 Friday

2000 2000 2000 2000 2000 2000 2000 2000 2000 2000 2000 2000 2000

Good Friday

Holiday
Rep. of Irela
and N. Irelar

22

Saturday

April

23

Sunday

April

* World Events

! My World

? Fact File

April

Easter
Sunday

2000 2000 2000 2000 2000 2000 2000 2000 2000 2000 2000 2000 2000

2000 2000 2000 2000 2000 2000 2000 2000 2000 2000 2000 2000 2000

2000 2000 2000 2000 2000 2000 2000 2000 2000 2000 2000 2000 2000

2000 2000 2000 2000 2000 2000 2000 2000 2000 2000 2000 2000 2000

2000 2000 2000 2000 2000 2000 2000 2000 2000 2000 2000 2000 2000

On 23 April 1014 Brian Boru's army defeated Máel
Mórda's army at the Battle of Clontarf. Brian Boru himself was killed during the battle, but his army's victory
meant the end of Viking rule in Ireland.

April

24 Monday

2000 2000 2000 2000 2000 2000 2000 2000 2000 2000 2000 2000 2000

Easter
Monday
Holiday

UK and Rep.
of Ireland

25 Tuesday

2000 2000 2000 2000 2000 2000 2000 2000 2000 2000 2000 2000 2000

26 Wednesday

2000 2000 2000 2000 2000 2000 2000 2000 2000 2000 2000 2000 2000

Last Quarter

27 Thursday

2000 2000 2000 2000 2000 2000 2000 2000 2000 2000 2000 2000 2000

28 Friday

2000 2000 2000 2000 2000 2000 2000 2000 2000 2000 2000 2000 2000

2000 2000 2000 2000 2000 2000 2000 2000 2000 2000 2000 2000 2000

2000 2000 2000 2000 2000 2000 2000 2000 2000 2000 2000 2000 2000

2000 2000 2000 2000 2000 2000 2000 2000 2000 2000 2000 2000 2000

2000 2000 2000 2000 2000 2000 2000 2000 2000 2000 2000 2000 2000

2000 2000 2000 2000 2000 2000 2000 2000 2000 2000 2000 2000 2000

29

Saturday

30

Sunday

* World Events

! My World

? Fact File

April April April

On 24 April 1916 the Easter Rising began. Over the five days of the Rising, 310 people were killed and Dublin was left in ruins. The rebel leaders, including Patrick Pearse and James Connolly, were later executed.

TELEVISION

In the future, television will probably change. Someday we may be using our TV screens for all kinds of things — ordering food or booking holidays. But right now, we use it to watch our favourite programmes. Whether it's Kids' TV or the news, everyone has something they love to watch.

I watch TV __ times a week.

I like to watch:

Cartoons	☐	Films	☐
Mini-Series	☐	Thrillers	☐
Soap Operas	☐	Nature Shows	☐
Comedies	☐	Science Fiction	☐
Chat Shows	☐	Game Shows	☐
News	☐	Other	☐

My favourite TV programme is
_____

This programme is about
_____
_____
_____
_____

My favourite character in this programme is
_____

I like this programme because
_____
_____
_____
_____
_____

MOVIES

Everybody loves the movies. We love going to the cinema to watch our favourite actors and actresses living wonderful on-screen lives. And there are so many types of movies, it's always difficult to decide which one to watch. Luckily, because of video recorders, we can watch movies over and over again in our own homes.

My favourite movie is called

_____

This movie is about

_____
_____
_____
_____
_____
_____

My favourite actor/actress is

_____

This is a picture of him/her:

Cut a picture out of a magazine or newspaper and paste it in here.

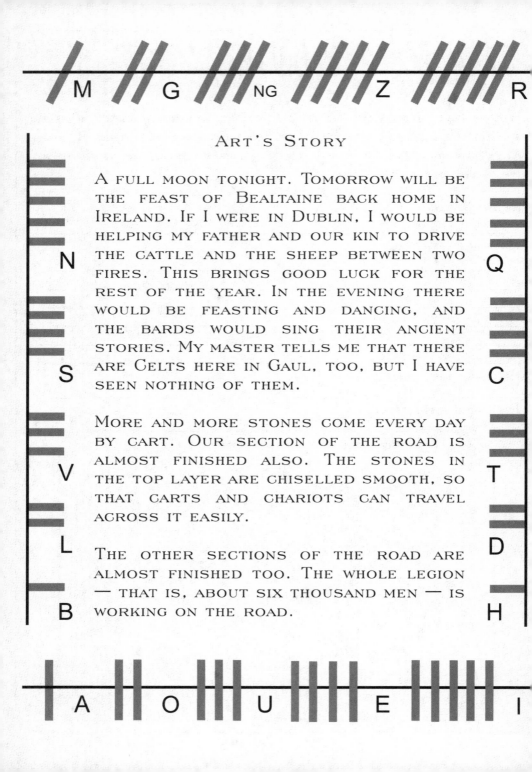

Art's Story

A full moon tonight. Tomorrow will be the feast of Bealtaine back home in Ireland. If I were in Dublin, I would be helping my father and our kin to drive the cattle and the sheep between two fires. This brings good luck for the rest of the year. In the evening there would be feasting and dancing, and the bards would sing their ancient stories. My master tells me that there are Celts here in Gaul, too, but I have seen nothing of them.

More and more stones come every day by cart. Our section of the road is almost finished also. The stones in the top layer are chiselled smooth, so that carts and chariots can travel across it easily.

The other sections of the road are almost finished too. The whole legion — that is, about six thousand men — is working on the road.

Finn's Story

Last night there was a full moon. I couldn't sleep. I heard a noise, so I went to the door of the house and looked down the street. All the houses in the street had May-bushes stuck outside them on poles. People say that it's to honour Mary, the mother of God, but the priests don't like it. They think it's too much like the old pagan festival of Bealtaine. When I looked at the house next to ours, I thought I saw the bush move and turn into the figure of a man. I rubbed my eyes and looked again, but there was only a bush there.

This morning, while we were eating our breakfast of porridge and herrings, Ita told me that she also heard a noise in the night. She said it sounded like the footsteps of a man.

May

01 Monday
2000 2000 2000 2000 2000 2000 2000 2000 2000 2000 2000 2000 2000

Holiday
UK and Rep.
of Ireland

02 Tuesday
2000 2000 2000 2000 2000 2000 2000 2000 2000 2000 2000 2000 2000

03 Wednesday
2000 2000 2000 2000 2000 2000 2000 2000 2000 2000 2000 2000 2000

04 Thursday
2000 2000 2000 2000 2000 2000 2000 2000 2000 2000 2000 2000 2000

New Moon

05 Friday
2000 2000 2000 2000 2000 2000 2000 2000 2000 2000 2000 2000 2000

06
Saturday

07
Sunday

May
May
mAY

* World Events
! My World
? Fact File

2000 2000 2000 2000 2000 2000 2000 2000 2000 2000 2000 2000 2000

2000 2000 2000 2000 2000 2000 2000 2000 2000 2000 2000 2000 2000

2000 2000 2000 2000 2000 2000 2000 2000 2000 2000 2000 2000 2000

2000 2000 2000 2000 2000 2000 2000 2000 2000 2000 2000 2000 2000

2000 2000 2000 2000 2000 2000 2000 2000 2000 2000 2000 2000 2000

On 7 May 1915 the *Lusitania* was torpedoed by a German U-boat off Kinsale. Over 1,000 people died, including the art collector Sir Hugh Lane. Some of his pictures were lost, but others are in the Hugh Lane Gallery in Dublin.

May

08 Monday

2000 2000 2000 2000 2000 2000 2000 2000 2000 2000 2000 2000 2000

May

09 Tuesday

2000 2000 2000 2000 2000 2000 2000 2000 2000 2000 2000 2000 2000

May

10 Wednesday

2000 2000 2000 2000 2000 2000 2000 2000 2000 2000 2000 2000 2000

First Quarter

11 Thursday

2000 2000 2000 2000 2000 2000 2000 2000 2000 2000 2000 2000 2000

May

12 Friday

2000 2000 2000 2000 2000 2000 2000 2000 2000 2000 2000 2000 2000

13 Saturday

14 Sunday

* World Events

! My World

? Fact File

May

May

mAy

2000 2000 2000 2000 2000 2000 2000 2000 2000 2000 2000 2000 2000

2000 2000 2000 2000 2000 2000 2000 2000 2000 2000 2000 2000 2000

2000 2000 2000 2000 2000 2000 2000 2000 2000 2000 2000 2000 2000

2000 2000 2000 2000 2000 2000 2000 2000 2000 2000 2000 2000 2000

2000 2000 2000 2000 2000 2000 2000 2000 2000 2000 2000 2000 2000

On 9 May 1671 Colonel Thomas Blood, an Irish adventurer, tried to steal the crown jewels. When he was arrested, he asked that the King hear the trial. Charles II pardoned him and gave him a pension of £500 a year!

May

15 Monday

2000 2000 2000 2000 2000 2000 2000 2000 2000 2000 2000 2000 2000

16 Tuesday

2000 2000 2000 2000 2000 2000 2000 2000 2000 2000 2000 2000 2000

17 Wednesday

2000 2000 2000 2000 2000 2000 2000 2000 2000 2000 2000 2000 2000

18 Thursday

2000 2000 2000 2000 2000 2000 2000 2000 2000 2000 2000 2000

Full Moon

Buddha's Birthday

19 Friday

2000 2000 2000 2000 2000 2000 2000 2000 2000 2000 2000 2000 2000

2000 2000 2000 2000 2000 2000 2000 2000 2000 2000 2000 2000 2000

2000 2000 2000 2000 2000 2000 2000 2000 2000 2000 2000 2000 2000

Gemini
21 May -
20 June

2000 2000 2000 2000 2000 2000 2000 2000 2000 2000 2000 2000 2000

2000 2000 2000 2000 2000 2000 2000 2000 2000 2000 2000 2000 2000

2000 2000 2000 2000 2000 2000 2000 2000 2000 2000 2000 2000 2000

On 20 May 1932 Amelia Earhart landed at Culmar, County Derry. She had flown from Newfoundland — 2,606 miles away — and was the first woman pilot to fly across the Atlantic alone. The flight took 13 hours.

20
Saturday
21
Sunday
May
*
World
Events
May
!
My World
?
Fact File
MAY

May

22 Monday
2000 2000 2000 2000 2000 2000 2000 2000 2000 2000 2000 2000 2000

23 Tuesday
2000 2000 2000 2000 2000 2000 2000 2000 2000 2000 2000 2000 2000

24 Wednesday
2000 2000 2000 2000 2000 2000 2000 2000 2000 2000 2000 2000 2000

25 Thursday
2000 2000 2000 2000 2000 2000 2000 2000 2000 2000 2000 2000 2000

26 Friday
2000 2000 2000 2000 2000 2000 2000 2000 2000 2000 2000 2000 2000

Last Quarter

2000 2000 2000 2000 2000 2000 2000 2000 2000 2000 2000 2000 2000

2000 2000 2000 2000 2000 2000 2000 2000 2000 2000 2000 2000 2000

2000 2000 2000 2000 2000 2000 2000 2000 2000 2000 2000 2000 2000

2000 2000 2000 2000 2000 2000 2000 2000 2000 2000 2000 2000 2000

2000 2000 2000 2000 2000 2000 2000 2000 2000 2000 2000 2000 2000

On 23 May 1798, rebellion broke out in Leinster. There was fighting in Naas, Clane and Rathangan.

27 Saturday May

28 Sunday May

* World Events

! My World

? Fact File

mAY

May

29 Monday

30 Tuesday

31 Wednesday

School's about to break up for the summer, and you'll be able to spend your time any way you like. Use this space to describe your perfect day. Who would you spend it with? Where would you go? What would you do?

May

15 Most Widely Spoken Languages

Language	Country	Population (millions)
1. Mandarin Chinese	China	885.0
2. Spanish	Spain, South America	332.0
3. English	UK, US, Australia	322.0
4. Bengali	Bangladesh	189.0
5. Hindi	India	182.0
6. Portuguese	Portugal, Brazil	170.0
7. Russian	Russia	170.0
8. Japanese	Japan	125.0
9. German	Germany	98.0
10. Wu Chinese	China	77.2
11. Javanese	Java, Indonesia	75.5
12. Korean	Korea	75.0
13. French	France, Switzerland, Canada	72.0
14. Vietnamese	Viet Nam	67.7
15. Telugu	India	66.4

2000 2000 2000 2000 2000 2000 2000 2000 2000 2000 2000 2000 2000

2000 2000 2000 2000 2000 2000 2000 2000 2000 2000 2000 2000 2000

2000 2000 2000 2000 2000 2000 2000 2000 2000 2000 2000 2000 2000

On 31 May 1941 a German pilot accidentally dropped a bomb on Dublin's North Strand. It killed over 30 people, injured 90 and left over 500 homeless. After the war, the German government paid compensation to victims and their relatives.

* World Events

! My World

? Fact File

THE ZODIAC

Signs of the Zodiac

Sign	Dates	Ruling Planet	Element	Symbol
Aries	21 March - 19 April	Mars	Fire	♈
Taurus	20 April - 20 May	Venus	Earth	♉
Gemini	21 May - 20 June	Mercury	Air	♊
Cancer	21 June - 22 July	Moon	Water	♋
Leo	23 July - 22 August	Sun	Fire	♌
Virgo	23 August - 22 September	Mercury	Earth	♍
Libra	23 September - 22 October	Venus	Air	♎
Scorpio	23 October - 21 November	Mars & Pluto	Water	♏
Sagittarius	22 November - 21 December	Jupiter	Fire	♐
Capricorn	22 December - 19 January	Saturn	Earth	♑
Aquarius	20 January - 18 February	Saturn & Uranus	Air	♒
Pisces	19 February - 20 March	Jupiter & Neptune	Water	♓

Month	Birthstone	Flower
January	Garnet	carnation
February	Amethyst	violet
March	Aquamarine or Bloodstone	jonquil
April	Diamond	sweet pea
May	Emerald	lily of the valley
June	Pearl, Alexandrite, or Moonstone	rose
July	Ruby or Star Ruby	larkspur
August	Peridot or Sardonyx	gladiolus
September	Sapphire or Star Sapphire	aster
October	Opal or Tourmaline	calendula
November	Topaz or Citrine	chrysanthemum
December	Turquoise, Lapis Lazuli, Blue Zircon, or Blue Topaz	narcissus

CHINESE ASTROLOGY

The 12 Animal Signs of Chinese Astrology

1	Rat
2	Ox
3	Tiger
4	Rabbit
5	Dragon
6	Snake
7	Horse
8	Goat
9	Monkey
10	Rooster
11	Dog
12	Pig

Animal Signs

The twelve animal signs are the basic foundation of Chinese astrology. The signs are based on the year in which you were born. The animals always follow the order shown opposite, and every twelve years the cycle starts all over again.

The calendar we use is based on the solar year, or the orbit of the Earth around the sun — that is, it takes the Earth approximately 365 days to orbit the sun. The Chinese calendar is different; it is based on the lunar year, or the moon's orbit around the Earth.

Below is a table of years and animal signs, so you can find out what your Chinese animal sign is!

2 February 1984—18 February 1996

1984	2	February	1984	—	19	February	1985	Rat
1985	20	Februsry	1985	—	8	February	1986	Ox
1986	9	February	1986	—	28	January	1987	Tiger
1987	29	January	1987	—	16	February	1988	Rabbit
1988	17	February	1988	—	5	February	1989	Dragon
1989	6	February	1989	—	26	January	1990	Snake
1990	27	January	1990	—	14	February	1991	Horse
1991	15	February	1991	—	3	February	1992	Goat
1992	4	Februasy	1992	—	22	January	1993	Monkey
1993	23	January	1993	—	9	February	1994	Rooster
1994	19	February	1994	—	30	January	1995	Dog
1995	31	January	1995	—	18	February	1996	Pig

Art's Story

The longest day of the year, the day of the summer solstice. In the distance I can see the fires of the Gaulish Celts. I think about my own home, beside the black pool which gave our place its name of Dublin. I wonder how I can escape and get back there.

Our road is finished. It is four paces wide and stretches as far as the eye can see, with neither a bend nor a curve in the whole length of it. In Ireland we make roads from planks of wood. If I ever get back, I will teach my people how to build roads of stone like these Romans do.

❖

Yesterday I went with my master to the house of a Roman tribune. Instead of having just one room, like our houses, it had many rooms — rooms for cooking, rooms for eating, rooms for sleeping.

Ita's Story

'By St John's Eve,' Father says, 'the boat will be finished.'
Mother is heating up pitch, which will be brushed between the
strakes so that not a drop of water can come through.

⌘

Today Father carved a dragon on the prow of the ship. Mother
is just finishing the sail. She wove it from linen threads and
dyed it red with the root of the madder plant.

⌘

The rudder has been fixed at the back of the ship. It's a long
stick, tied on with a piece of leather. It's there to steer the ship.

⌘

Tomorrow we'll test the new ship. Father's five brothers will
come with us, to row, and Finn and I will have an oar each as
well. We'll sit at the front of the boat, and Mother will stand
at the back and steer with the rudder.

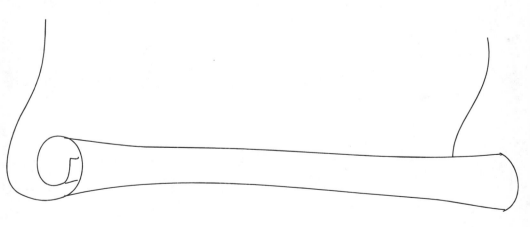

2000 2000 2000 2000 2000 2000 2000 2000 2000 2000 2000 2000 2000

The Planets in our Solar System

	Distance from Sun min. (Mkm) max.		Diameter (km)	Number of Moons
Mercury	46.8	- 69.4	4,878	0
Venus	107.6	- 109	12,104	0
Earth	147.4	- 152.6	12,756	1
Mars	207.3	- 249.2	6,794	2
Jupiter	741.6	- 817.4	142,800	16
Saturn	1346	- 1512	120,000	17
Uranus	2740	- 3011	52,000	15
Neptune	4466	- 4543	48,400	8
Pluto	4461	- 7364	1,145	1

2000 2000 2000 2000 2000 2000 2000 2000 2000 2000 2000 2000 2000

01

Thursday

Ascension
Day

2000 2000 2000 2000 2000 2000 2000 2000 2000 2000 2000 2000 2000

02

Friday

New Moon

03
Saturday

04
Sunday

*
World Events

!
My World

?
Fact File

June June June

2000 2000 2000 2000 2000 2000 2000 2000 2000 2000 2000 2000 2000

2000 2000 2000 2000 2000 2000 2000 2000 2000 2000 2000 2000 2000

2000 2000 2000 2000 2000 2000 2000 2000 2000 2000 2000 2000 2000

2000 2000 2000 2000 2000 2000 2000 2000 2000 2000 2000 2000 2000

2000 2000 2000 2000 2000 2000 2000 2000 2000 2000 2000 2000 2000

On 1 June 1852 a telegraph cable was run under the sea from Holyhead to Howth, linking Britain and Ireland for the first time.

June

05 Monday

2000 2000 2000 2000 2000 2000 2000 2000 2000 2000 2000 2000 2000

Holiday
Rep. of Ireland

06 Tuesday

2000 2000 2000 2000 2000 2000 2000 2000 2000 2000 2000 2000 2000

07 Wednesday

2000 2000 2000 2000 2000 2000 2000 2000 2000 2000 2000 2000 2000

08 Thursday

2000 2000 2000 2000 2000 2000 2000 2000 2000 2000 2000 2000 2000

09 Friday

2000 2000 2000 2000 2000 2000 2000 2000 2000 2000 2000 2000 2000

First Quarter

_2000 2000 2000 2000 2000 2000 2000 2000 2000 2000 2000 2000 2000_

Pentecost

_2000 2000 2000 2000 2000 2000 2000 2000 2000 2000 2000 2000 2000_

_2000 2000 2000 2000 2000 2000 2000 2000 2000 2000 2000 2000 2000_

_2000 2000 2000 2000 2000 2000 2000 2000 2000 2000 2000 2000 2000_

_2000 2000 2000 2000 2000 2000 2000 2000 2000 2000 2000 2000 2000_

On 5 June 1646, at the Battle of Benburb in County Tyrone, Owen Roe O'Neill's soldiers defeated the English and Scottish soldiers led by Robert Monroe.

10 Saturday

11 Sunday

June

* World Events

June

! My World

? Fact File

June

June

12 Monday

2000 2000 2000 2000 2000 2000 2000 2000 2000 2000 2000 2000 2000

13 Tuesday

2000 2000 2000 2000 2000 2000 2000 2000 2000 2000 2000 2000 2000

14 Wednesday

2000 2000 2000 2000 2000 2000 2000 2000 2000 2000 2000 2000 2000

15 Thursday

2000 2000 2000 2000 2000 2000 2000 2000 2000 2000 2000 2000 2000

16 Friday

2000 2000 2000 2000 2000 2000 2000 2000 2000 2000 2000 2000 2000

Full Moon

17

Saturday

18

Sunday

*

World Events

!

My World

?

Fact File

June   June   June

2000 2000 2000 2000 2000 2000 2000 2000 2000 2000 2000 2000 2000

2000 2000 2000 2000 2000 2000 2000 2000 2000 2000 2000 2000 2000

Father's Day

2000 2000 2000 2000 2000 2000 2000 2000 2000 2000 2000 2000 2000

2000 2000 2000 2000 2000 2000 2000 2000 2000 2000 2000 2000 2000

2000 2000 2000 2000 2000 2000 2000 2000 2000 2000 2000 2000 2000

On 13 June 1699 Molly Malone, the famous Dublin fishmonger, was buried. She was 29 when she died.

June

19 Monday

2000 2000 2000 2000 2000 2000 2000 2000 2000 2000 2000 2000 2000

20 Tuesday

2000 2000 2000 2000 2000 2000 2000 2000 2000 2000 2000 2000 2000

21 Wednesday

2000 2000 2000 2000 2000 2000 2000 2000 2000 2000 2000 2000 2000

Cancer
21 June -
22 July

22 Thursday

2000 2000 2000 2000 2000 2000 2000 2000 2000 2000 2000 2000 2000

Corpus
Christi

23 Friday

2000 2000 2000 2000 2000 2000 2000 2000 2000 2000 2000 2000 2000

2000 2000 2000 2000 2000 2000 2000 2000 2000 2000 2000 2000 2000

Last Quarter

2000 2000 2000 2000 2000 2000 2000 2000 2000 2000 2000 2000 2000

2000 2000 2000 2000 2000 2000 2000 2000 2000 2000 2000 2000 2000

2000 2000 2000 2000 2000 2000 2000 2000 2000 2000 2000 2000 2000

2000 2000 2000 2000 2000 2000 2000 2000 2000 2000 2000 2000 2000

On 25 June 1959 Eamon De Valera became the third President of Ireland. On the same date in 1973 Erskine Childers took up office as the fourth President.

24 Saturday June

25 Sunday June

* World Events

! My World

? Fact File

June

26
June
Monday

2000 2000 2000 2000 2000 2000 2000 2000 2000 2000 2000 2000 2000

27
Tuesday

2000 2000 2000 2000 2000 2000 2000 2000 2000 2000 2000 2000 2000

28
June
Wednesday

2000 2000 2000 2000 2000 2000 2000 2000 2000 2000 2000 2000 2000

29
Thursday

2000 2000 2000 2000 2000 2000 2000 2000 2000 2000 2000 2000 2000

30
June
Friday

2000 2000 2000 2000 2000 2000 2000 2000 2000 2000 2000 2000 2000

The NATO alphabet is the system used by armies, navies, air forces and airlines the world over. It makes radio communication simpler for everyone involved, because if you spell words out using the ordinary alphabet, many letters sound the same (D and T, for example), which can lead to confusion. You've probably heard the NATO alphabet on TV or in the movies, so here's your own copy....

A - Alpha	H - Hotel	O - Oscar	V - Victor
B - Beta	I - India	P - Papa	W - Whisky
C - Charlie	J - Juliet	Q - Quebec	X - X-Ray
D - Delta	K - Kilo	R - Romeo	Y - Yankee
E - Echo	L - Lima	S - Sierra	Z - Zulu
F - Foxtrot	M - Mike	T - Tango	
G - Golf	N - November	U - Uniform	

2000 2000 2000 2000 2000 2000 2000 2000 2000 2000 2000 2000 2000

2000 2000 2000 2000 2000 2000 2000 2000 2000 2000 2000 2000 2000

2000 2000 2000 2000 2000 2000 2000 2000 2000 2000 2000 2000 2000

On 27 June 1846 Charles Stewart Parnell was born in Avondale, County Wicklow. He was to become the leading figure in Ireland's fight for Home Rule.

June

June

June

June

* World Events

! My World

? Fact File

BOOKS

My favourite book is called _____

It was written by _____

My favourite character in the book is _____

Other books I like are _____

_____

_____

Below is the story of my favourite book.

_____

_____

_____

_____

_____

_____

_____

_____

_____

_____

_____

_____

_____

_____

M   G   NG   Z   R

Art's Story

N

Today I went to the Roman house again. I tasted the fruit of the vines that grow in the fields around it. These grapes are sweet, but wine, the drink that they make from them, is sour. I prefer mead, which we make from honey. The house is very beautiful, though. The floors are made from a stone called marble, and the floors and walls have pictures on them, made from tiny cubes of different-coloured marbles.

S

❖

Yesterday my master told me that, when one more month has passed, the legion will return to Rome. 'What about me?' I asked. 'You will go with us,' he replied.

V

I must escape and return to my own people. But how? Perhaps I could climb on board one of the ships in the harbour and hide there. These days my master allows me to wander where I wish. He has said that I am a good worker.

L

B

Q

C

T

D

H

A   O   U   E   I

Finn's Story

We've been too sad to write for days and days. On St John's Eve we went down the Liffey and towards the sea in the splendid new ship, and it tipped over onto one side!

Father has spent days in the alehouse. All the money his brothers have lent him will soon be gone.

The shoemaker's daughter has come back to live in Dublin. Her husband, the boat-builder, has come with her.

⌘

Ita and I went down to the riverside today. The shoemaker and his daughter's husband and other people from his kin-group are building a new house there. We watched them. They've collected a huge pile of hazel rods for the walls. They were hammering the four corner-posts into the ground. It will be a big house. It must measure about three of a man's paces long and two paces wide.

2000 2000 2000 2000 2000 2000 2000 2000 2000 2000 2000 2000 2000

2000 2000 2000 2000 2000 2000 2000 2000 2000 2000 2000 2000 2000

2000 2000 2000 2000 2000 2000 2000 2000 2000 2000 2000 2000 2000

2000 2000 2000 2000 2000 2000 2000 2000 2000 2000 2000 2000 2000

2000 2000 2000 2000 2000 2000 2000 2000 2000 2000 2000 2000 2000

On 1 July 1690, the army of William of Orange defeated James II and his army at the Battle of the Boyne.

01 Saturday July

02 Sunday

* World Events July

! My World

? Fact File July

Monday

2000 2000 2000 2000 2000 2000 2000 2000 2000 2000 2000 2000 2000

יולי

04

Tuesday

2000 2000 2000 2000 2000 2000 2000 2000 2000 2000 2000 2000 2000

05

Wednesday

2000 2000 2000 2000 2000 2000 2000 2000 2000 2000 2000 2000 2000

יולי

06

Thursday

2000 2000 2000 2000 2000 2000 2000 2000 2000 2000 2000 2000 2000

07

Friday

2000 2000 2000 2000 2000 2000 2000 2000 2000 2000 2000 2000 2000

יולי

First Quarter

2000 2000 2000 2000 2000 2000 2000 2000 2000 2000 2000 2000 2000

08

Saturday

2000 2000 2000 2000 2000 2000 2000 2000 2000 2000 2000 2000 2000

09

Sunday

*

2000 2000 2000 2000 2000 2000 2000 2000 2000 2000 2000 2000 2000

World Events

!

2000 2000 2000 2000 2000 2000 2000 2000 2000 2000 2000 2000 2000

My World

?

2000 2000 2000 2000 2000 2000 2000 2000 2000 2000 2000 2000 2000

On 6 July 1907 the Irish crown jewels disappeared from Dublin Castle. They have never been found. The jewels were worth £50,000 in 1907.

Fact File

July

10 Monday

2000 2000 2000 2000 2000 2000 2000 2000 2000 2000 2000 2000 2000

11 Tuesday

2000 2000 2000 2000 2000 2000 2000 2000 2000 2000 2000 2000 2000

July

12 Wednesday

2000 2000 2000 2000 2000 2000 2000 2000 2000 2000 2000 2000 2000

Holiday
N. Ireland

13 Thursday

2000 2000 2000 2000 2000 2000 2000 2000 2000 2000 2000 2000 2000

July

14 Friday

2000 2000 2000 2000 2000 2000 2000 2000 2000 2000 2000 2000 2000

Full Moon

2000 2000 2000 2000 2000 2000 2000 2000 2000 2000 2000 2000 2000

2000 2000 2000 2000 2000 2000 2000 2000 2000 2000 2000 2000 2000

2000 2000 2000 2000 2000 2000 2000 2000 2000 2000 2000 2000 2000

2000 2000 2000 2000 2000 2000 2000 2000 2000 2000 2000 2000 2000

2000 2000 2000 2000 2000 2000 2000 2000 2000 2000 2000 2000 2000

On 15 July 1865 it was discovered that 'Dr James Barry', Chief Medical Officer in the British Army, was really the daughter of a Corkman. She had spent her life pretending to be a man so that she could be a doctor.

17

Monday

2000 2000 2000 2000 2000 2000 2000 2000 2000 2000 2000 2000 2000

18

Tuesday

2000 2000 2000 2000 2000 2000 2000 2000 2000 2000 2000 2000 2000

19

Wednesday

2000 2000 2000 2000 2000 2000 2000 2000 2000 2000 2000 2000 2000

20

Thursday

2000 2000 2000 2000 2000 2000 2000 2000 2000 2000 2000 2000 2000

21

Friday

2000 2000 2000 2000 2000 2000 2000 2000 2000 2000 2000 2000 2000

2000 2000 2000 2000 2000 2000 2000 2000 2000 2000 2000 2000 2000

2000 2000 2000 2000 2000 2000 2000 2000 2000 2000 2000 2000 2000

2000 2000 2000 2000 2000 2000 2000 2000 2000 2000 2000 2000 2000

2000 2000 2000 2000 2000 2000 2000 2000 2000 2000 2000 2000 2000

2000 2000 2000 2000 2000 2000 2000 2000 2000 2000 2000 2000 2000

On 23 July 1803 Robert Emmet led a small rising in Thomas Street, Dublin. The rising failed, and Robert Emmet was later arrested, tried and hanged.

22 Saturday July

23 Sunday July

* World Events July

! My World

? Fact File July

24
July
Monday

2000 2000 2000 2000 2000 2000 2000 2000 2000 2000 2000 2000 2000

25
Tuesday

2000 2000 2000 2000 2000 2000 2000 2000 2000 2000 2000 2000 2000

26
July
Wednesday

2000 2000 2000 2000 2000 2000 2000 2000 2000 2000 2000 2000 2000

27
Thursday

2000 2000 2000 2000 2000 2000 2000 2000 2000 2000 2000 2000 2000

28
July
Friday

2000 2000 2000 2000 2000 2000 2000 2000 2000 2000 2000 2000 2000

2000 2000 2000 2000 2000 2000 2000 2000 2000 2000 2000 2000 2000

2000 2000 2000 2000 2000 2000 2000 2000 2000 2000 2000 2000 2000

2000 2000 2000 2000 2000 2000 2000 2000 2000 2000 2000 2000 2000

2000 2000 2000 2000 2000 2000 2000 2000 2000 2000 2000 2000 2000

2000 2000 2000 2000 2000 2000 2000 2000 2000 2000 2000 2000 2000

On 26 July 1856 George Bernard Shaw was born. He went on to become a great playwright. In 1925 he won the Nobel Prize for Literature.

2000 2000 2000 2000 2000 2000 2000 2000 2000 2000 2000 2000 2000

New Moon

2000 2000 2000 2000 2000 2000 2000 2000 2000 2000 2000 2000 2000

Food Facts

Most people associate potatoes with Ireland. Although they are our main crop, the potato originally comes from Peru; it was brought to Europe by explorers.

***

French fries do not come from France. They were first made in Belgium in 1876. The word 'French' refers to the way of cutting the potatoes before cooking them.

2000 2000 2000 2000 2000 2000 2000 2000 2000 2000 2000 2000 2000

World Events

2000 2000 2000 2000 2000 2000 2000 2000 2000 2000 2000 2000 2000

My World

2000 2000 2000 2000 2000 2000 2000 2000 2000 2000 2000 2000 2000

Fact File

On 31 July 1893 Conradh na Gaeilge (the Gaelic League) was founded to protect the Irish language. One of its founders was Douglas Hyde, who later became the first President of Ireland.

MY SUMMER 2000

Paste in a photo from your first holiday of the millennium!

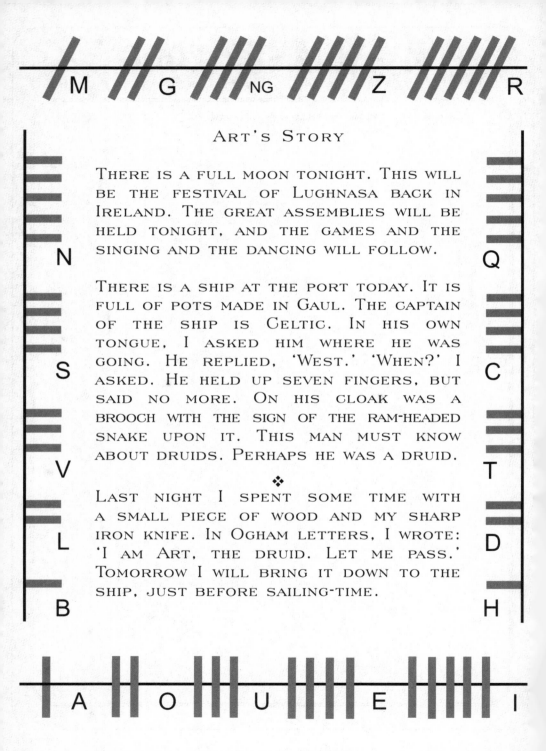

ART'S STORY

THERE IS A FULL MOON TONIGHT. THIS WILL BE THE FESTIVAL OF LUGHNASA BACK IN IRELAND. THE GREAT ASSEMBLIES WILL BE HELD TONIGHT, AND THE GAMES AND THE SINGING AND THE DANCING WILL FOLLOW.

THERE IS A SHIP AT THE PORT TODAY. IT IS FULL OF POTS MADE IN GAUL. THE CAPTAIN OF THE SHIP IS CELTIC. IN HIS OWN TONGUE, I ASKED HIM WHERE HE WAS GOING. HE REPLIED, 'WEST.' 'WHEN?' I ASKED. HE HELD UP SEVEN FINGERS, BUT SAID NO MORE. ON HIS CLOAK WAS A BROOCH WITH THE SIGN OF THE RAM-HEADED SNAKE UPON IT. THIS MAN MUST KNOW ABOUT DRUIDS. PERHAPS HE WAS A DRUID.

❖

LAST NIGHT I SPENT SOME TIME WITH A SMALL PIECE OF WOOD AND MY SHARP IRON KNIFE. IN OGHAM LETTERS, I WROTE: 'I AM ART, THE DRUID. LET ME PASS.' TOMORROW I WILL BRING IT DOWN TO THE SHIP, JUST BEFORE SAILING-TIME.

Ita's Story

My father is still drinking in the alehouse. Mother spends her time crying and praying in the church of St Olave. Every day Finn and I go fishing. Today we caught a lot of herrings. They'll feed us for the week, so we won't starve this week, at least.

Every day we look at the splendid boat, now lying in the yard outside our house. 'What went wrong?' we keep asking ourselves. 'Why did it tip over like that?'

⌘

We went down to see the new house again today. They've done a lot of work during the week. The four walls, made of woven hazel rods, have been nailed to the four corner-posts. Two men were collecting liquid mud from the river in baskets and smearing it thickly onto the woven hazel of the walls. This will be a warm, draught-free house.

'Who will live there?' Finn asked the shoemaker.

'My daughter and her husband, of course,' he answered. Finn and I looked at each other.

01 Tuesday
02 Wednesday
03 Thursday
04 Friday

2000 2000 2000 2000 2000 2000 2000 2000 2000 2000 2000 2000 2000

Food Facts
One of our favourite Chinese foods, chop suey, was created in America by a Chinese cook in the 1800s. He stir-fried a mixture of vegetables and called it 'tsa sui' — Mandarin Chinese for 'various things' — which people said as 'chop suey'!

***

Although ice-cream feels cold, it is loaded with calories (units of heat) and actually makes your body warmer!

2000 2000 2000 2000 2000 2000 2000 2000 2000 2000 2000 2000 2000

2000 2000 2000 2000 2000 2000 2000 2000 2000 2000 2000 2000 2000

2000 2000 2000 2000 2000 2000 2000 2000 2000 2000 2000 2000 2000

2000 2000 2000 2000 2000 2000 2000 2000 2000 2000 2000 2000 2000

05

Saturday

August

06

Sunday

*

World
Events

!

My World

?

Fact File

August

August

2000 2000 2000 2000 2000 2000 2000 2000 2000 2000 2000 2000 2000

2000 2000 2000 2000 2000 2000 2000 2000 2000 2000 2000 2000 2000

2000 2000 2000 2000 2000 2000 2000 2000 2000 2000 2000 2000 2000

2000 2000 2000 2000 2000 2000 2000 2000 2000 2000 2000 2000 2000

2000 2000 2000 2000 2000 2000 2000 2000 2000 2000 2000 2000 2000

On 6 August 1775 Daniel O'Connell was born in Cahirciveen, County Kerry. He was known as 'The Liberator' because he won rights and freedom for Irish Catholics.

August

07 Monday

2000 2000 2000 2000 2000 2000 2000 2000 2000 2000 2000 2000 2000

First Quarter

Holiday
Rep. of Ireland

08 Tuesday

2000 2000 2000 2000 2000 2000 2000 2000 2000 2000 2000 2000 2000

09 Wednesday

2000 2000 2000 2000 2000 2000 2000 2000 2000 2000 2000 2000 2000

10 Thursday

2000 2000 2000 2000 2000 2000 2000 2000 2000 2000 2000 2000 2000

11 Friday

2000 2000 2000 2000 2000 2000 2000 2000 2000 2000 2000 2000 2000

2000 2000 2000 2000 2000 2000 2000 2000 2000 2000 2000 2000 2000

2000 2000 2000 2000 2000 2000 2000 2000 2000 2000 2000 2000 2000

2000 2000 2000 2000 2000 2000 2000 2000 2000 2000 2000 2000 2000

2000 2000 2000 2000 2000 2000 2000 2000 2000 2000 2000 2000 2000

2000 2000 2000 2000 2000 2000 2000 2000 2000 2000 2000 2000 2000

On 8 August 1992 Michael Carruth from Dublin won a gold medal for boxing at the Olympic Games in Barcelona.

12 August
Saturday

13 August
Sunday

* August
World Events

! August
My World

? August
Fact File

August

14 Monday

2000 2000 2000 2000 2000 2000 2000 2000 2000 2000 2000 2000 2000

15 Tuesday

2000 2000 2000 2000 2000 2000 2000 2000 2000 2000 2000 2000 2000

Full Moon

16 Wednesday

2000 2000 2000 2000 2000 2000 2000 2000 2000 2000 2000 2000 2000

17 Thursday

2000 2000 2000 2000 2000 2000 2000 2000 2000 2000 2000 2000 2000

18 Friday

2000 2000 2000 2000 2000 2000 2000 2000 2000 2000 2000 2000 2000

2000 2000 2000 2000 2000 2000 2000 2000 2000 2000 2000 2000 2000

2000 2000 2000 2000 2000 2000 2000 2000 2000 2000 2000 2000 2000

2000 2000 2000 2000 2000 2000 2000 2000 2000 2000 2000 2000 2000

2000 2000 2000 2000 2000 2000 2000 2000 2000 2000 2000 2000 2000

2000 2000 2000 2000 2000 2000 2000 2000 2000 2000 2000 2000 2000

19 Saturday

20 Sunday

* World Events

! My World

? Fact File

On 15 August 1649 Oliver Cromwell landed at Ringsend in Dublin with an army of 12,000 troops. During Cromwell's ten months in Ireland, many Catholics were killed or driven from their homes.

21
Monday

2000 2000 2000 2000 2000 2000 2000 2000 2000 2000 2000 2000 2000

22
Tuesday

2000 2000 2000 2000 2000 2000 2000 2000 2000 2000 2000 2000 2000

Last Quarter

Janamashtam

23
Wednesday

2000 2000 2000 2000 2000 2000 2000 2000 2000 2000 2000 2000 2000

24
Thursday

2000 2000 2000 2000 2000 2000 2000 2000 2000 2000 2000 2000 2000

25
Friday

2000 2000 2000 2000 2000 2000 2000 2000 2000 2000 2000 2000 2000

26 August
Saturday

27 August
Sunday

* World Events

! My World

? Fact File

August August August August

2000 2000 2000 2000 2000 2000 2000 2000 2000 2000 2000 2000 2000

2000 2000 2000 2000 2000 2000 2000 2000 2000 2000 2000 2000 2000

2000 2000 2000 2000 2000 2000 2000 2000 2000 2000 2000 2000 2000

2000 2000 2000 2000 2000 2000 2000 2000 2000 2000 2000 2000 2000

2000 2000 2000 2000 2000 2000 2000 2000 2000 2000 2000 2000 2000

On 23 August 1170 Strongbow landed at Passage, County Waterford, with his army. His real name was Richard FitzGilbert de Clare.

August

28 Monday

2000 2000 2000 2000 2000 2000 2000 2000 2000 2000 2000 2000 2000

Holiday
UK and
N. Ireland

29 Tuesday

2000 2000 2000 2000 2000 2000 2000 2000 2000 2000 2000 2000 2000

New Moon

30 Wednesday

2000 2000 2000 2000 2000 2000 2000 2000 2000 2000 2000 2000 2000

31 Thursday

2000 2000 2000 2000 2000 2000 2000 2000 2000 2000 2000 2000 2000

2000 2000 2000 2000 2000 2000 2000 2000 2000 2000 2000 2000 2000

Did you know?

A thousand years ago, Dublin was called 'Dyflin', which comes from the Irish 'Dubh Linn', meaning 'black pool'. The dark pool which gave the city its name is now covered over, but it was near where Dublin Castle stands today.

Did you know?

The nursery rhyme 'Ring-a-ring-a-rosy' dates back to the time of the Black Death. It describes the symptoms of the plague:

'Ring-a-ring-of-roses' — the circle of red spots that appeared on victims' foreheads

'a pocketful of posies' — the bunches of herbs and flowers people carried to ward off the plague

'atishoo, atishoo' — the sneezing that came with the illness

'we all fall down' — people falling down ill or dead

2000 2000 2000 2000 2000 2000 2000 2000 2000 2000 2000 2000 2000

2000 2000 2000 2000 2000 2000 2000 2000 2000 2000 2000 2000 2000

2000 2000 2000 2000 2000 2000 2000 2000 2000 2000 2000 2000 2000

On 31 August 1601 Red Hugh O'Donnell died in Spain of poisoning. He was chief of the O'Donnells of Donegal and had been an ally of Hugh O'Neill at the time of the Ulster Plantations.

August

August

August

August

* World Events

! My World

? Fact File

FRIENDS FOREVER

Who's sharing the first year of the new millennium with you? On this page, write something about each of your best friends, or glue in photos of them, or a photo of all of you together.

FRIENDS FOREVER

Get each of your best friends to write you a message on this page.

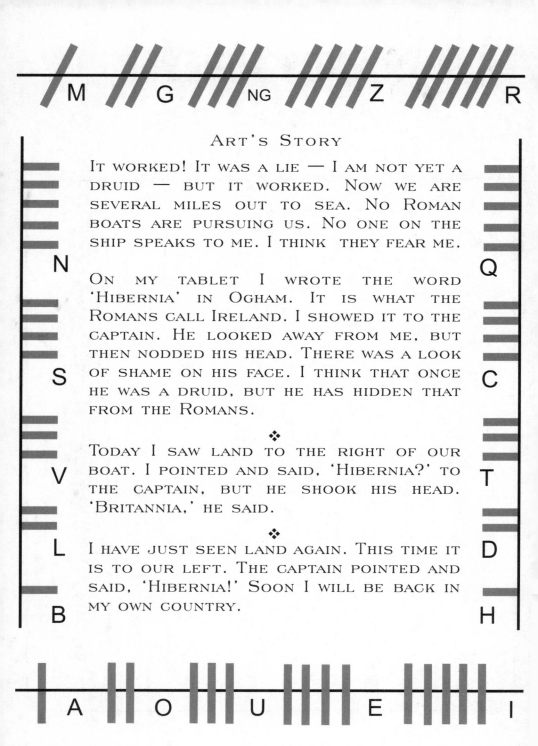

Art's Story

It worked! It was a lie — I am not yet a druid — but it worked. Now we are several miles out to sea. No Roman boats are pursuing us. No one on the ship speaks to me. I think they fear me.

On my tablet I wrote the word 'Hibernia' in Ogham. It is what the Romans call Ireland. I showed it to the captain. He looked away from me, but then nodded his head. There was a look of shame on his face. I think that once he was a druid, but he has hidden that from the Romans.

❖

Today I saw land to the right of our boat. I pointed and said, 'Hibernia?' to the captain, but he shook his head. 'Britannia,' he said.

❖

I have just seen land again. This time it is to our left. The captain pointed and said, 'Hibernia!' Soon I will be back in my own country.

Finn's Story

We went to see Olaf, the comb-maker, today. He makes his combs from deer's antlers, and he often gives us some of the leftover scraps, or carves them into gaming-pieces for us. While we were there, a drunken man came in and tried to steal some silver from Olaf. Quickly Olaf pulled off his shoe and hit the man on the head with the heel of it! The man staggered out of the shop and fell down on the wattle-covered pathway outside.

'How did you manage to hit him so hard?' I asked. Olaf smiled. 'Ivar the shoemaker stitched some lead into the heel of my shoe,' he said. 'He stitched it so cleverly that no one would know it's there.'

'If Ivar wants his daughter's husband to sell boats here in Dublin, he might try and wreck our father's boats,' Ita said to me later. 'Do you think he put lead in them, like he did in Olaf's shoe?'

Clothes

What's the fashion in the first year of the third millennium? Describe what you're wearing, or draw a picture of one of your favourite pieces of clothing, or glue in a photo of you in your favourite outfit.

September September September September September

01

Friday

02 September September September September

Saturday

03

Sunday

*

World
Events

!

My World

?

Fact File

2000 2000 2000 2000 2000 2000 2000 2000 2000 2000 2000 2000 2000

2000 2000 2000 2000 2000 2000 2000 2000 2000 2000 2000 2000 2000

2000 2000 2000 2000 2000 2000 2000 2000 2000 2000 2000 2000 2000

2000 2000 2000 2000 2000 2000 2000 2000 2000 2000 2000 2000 2000

2000 2000 2000 2000 2000 2000 2000 2000 2000 2000 2000 2000 2000

On 1 September 1864 Roger Casement was born in Dublin. He spent 20 years in the British Colonial Service and was knighted in 1911. In 1916 he was hanged in England for his part in the fight for Irish independence.

04

Monday

2000 2000 2000 2000 2000 2000 2000 2000 2000 2000 2000 2000 2000

05

Tuesday

2000 2000 2000 2000 2000 2000 2000 2000 2000 2000 2000 2000 2000

First Quarter

06

Wednesday

2000 2000 2000 2000 2000 2000 2000 2000 2000 2000 2000 2000 2000

07

Thursday

2000 2000 2000 2000 2000 2000 2000 2000 2000 2000 2000 2000 2000

08

Friday

2000 2000 2000 2000 2000 2000 2000 2000 2000 2000 2000 2000 2000

On 6 September 1987 Stephen Roche became the first Irish cyclist to win the World Professional Road Race Championship. In July of the same year he had won the Tour de France.

09 Saturday
10 Sunday
* World Events
! My World
? Fact File

September September September September September

11

Monday

2000 2000 2000 2000 2000 2000 2000 2000 2000 2000 2000 2000 2000

12

Tuesday

2000 2000 2000 2000 2000 2000 2000 2000 2000 2000 2000 2000 2000

13

Wednesday

2000 2000 2000 2000 2000 2000 2000 2000 2000 2000 2000 2000 2000

Full Moon

14

Thursday

2000 2000 2000 2000 2000 2000 2000 2000 2000 2000 2000 2000 2000

15

Friday

2000 2000 2000 2000 2000 2000 2000 2000 2000 2000 2000 2000 2000

2000 2000 2000 2000 2000 2000 2000 2000 2000 2000 2000 2000 2000

2000 2000 2000 2000 2000 2000 2000 2000 2000 2000 2000 2000 2000

2000 2000 2000 2000 2000 2000 2000 2000 2000 2000 2000 2000 2000

2000 2000 2000 2000 2000 2000 2000 2000 2000 2000 2000 2000 2000

2000 2000 2000 2000 2000 2000 2000 2000 2000 2000 2000 2000 2000

On 17 September 1862 the Battle of Antietam Creek took place in the American Civil War. Thomas Francis Meagher led the Irish Brigade. At the end of the day, 540 soldiers of this Brigade had been killed or injured.

16 Saturday

17 Sunday

September September September September

* World Events

! My World

? Fact File

September September September September September September September

18
Monday
2000 2000 2000 2000 2000 2000 2000 2000 2000 2000 2000 2000 2000

19
Tuesday
2000 2000 2000 2000 2000 2000 2000 2000 2000 2000 2000 2000 2000

20
Wednesday
2000 2000 2000 2000 2000 2000 2000 2000 2000 2000 2000 2000 2000

21
Thursday
2000 2000 2000 2000 2000 2000 2000 2000 2000 2000 2000 2000 2000

Last Quarter

22
Friday
2000 2000 2000 2000 2000 2000 2000 2000 2000 2000 2000 2000 2000

2000 2000 2000 2000 2000 2000 2000 2000 2000 2000 2000 2000 2000

2000 2000 2000 2000 2000 2000 2000 2000 2000 2000 2000 2000 2000

2000 2000 2000 2000 2000 2000 2000 2000 2000 2000 2000 2000 2000

2000 2000 2000 2000 2000 2000 2000 2000 2000 2000 2000 2000 2000

2000 2000 2000 2000 2000 2000 2000 2000 2000 2000 2000 2000 2000

On 18 September 1851 Anne Devlin died of starvation in Dublin. She had been Robert Emmet's housemaid and a committed rebel. She had been arrested and tortured and had spent three years in Kilmainham Gaol.

23 Saturday

24 Sunday

* World Events

! My World

? Fact File

25 Monday

2000 2000 2000 2000 2000 2000 2000 2000 2000 2000 2000 2000 2000

26 Tuesday

2000 2000 2000 2000 2000 2000 2000 2000 2000 2000 2000 2000 2000

27 Wednesday

2000 2000 2000 2000 2000 2000 2000 2000 2000 2000 2000 2000 2000

New Moon

28 Thursday

2000 2000 2000 2000 2000 2000 2000 2000 2000 2000 2000 2000 2000

29 Friday

2000 2000 2000 2000 2000 2000 2000 2000 2000 2000 2000 2000 2000

Rosh
Hashanah

2000 2000 2000 2000 2000 2000 2000 2000 2000 2000 2000 2000 2000

2000 2000 2000 2000 2000 2000 2000 2000 2000 2000 2000 2000 2000

Did you know?

The first ever public performance of Handel's *Messiah* was given in Dublin's Musick Hall on Fishamble Street in 1742.

2000 2000 2000 2000 2000 2000 2000 2000 2000 2000 2000 2000 2000

2000 2000 2000 2000 2000 2000 2000 2000 2000 2000 2000 2000 2000

2000 2000 2000 2000 2000 2000 2000 2000 2000 2000 2000 2000 2000

On 29 September 1979 Pope John Paul II arrived in Ireland. He was the first pope to visit Ireland, and he stayed for three days.

BACK TO SCHOOL

You've been back in school for a month now. What is school like in the first year of the new millennium? On this page you can write about school, or draw a picture of your teacher, or maybe even copy something out of your homework copybook.

Art's Story

I HAVE ARRIVED BACK IN MY OWN COUNTRY! MY MOTHER ALMOST FAINTED FROM JOY WHEN SHE SAW ME. A PIG WAS KILLED AND WE FEASTED ON ITS MEAT.

THIS MORNING ONE OF MY BROTHERS HELPED ME TO TAKE A BATH. WE LIT A FIRE BESIDE A SMALL POOL, HEATED STONES IN THE FIRE AND THREW THE HOT STONES INTO THE WATER. WHEN THE WATER WAS HOT ENOUGH, I GOT IN AND RUBBED MYSELF ALL OVER WITH THE SOAP WHICH MY MOTHER MAKES FROM ASHES AND THE SOAPWORT PLANT. I HAVE NOT HAD A BATH FOR SIX MONTHS. THE ROMANS HAD THEIR MAGNIFICENT BATH-HOUSES, WITH WATER HEATED BY GREAT FIRES UNDER-GROUND, BUT I, A SLAVE, WAS NOT ALLOWED TO USE THOSE BATHS.

THE HARVEST OF OATS AND DRIED BLACKBERRIES HAS BEEN STORED IN THE UNDERGROUND ROOM IN THE MIDDLE OF OUR ENCLOSURE. TODAY I HELPED MY BROTHERS TO GATHER HAZELNUTS TO STORE THERE ALSO.

M G NG Z R

N S V L B

Q C T D H

A O U E I

Ita's Story

Finn and I have spent seven days looking at the boat. If Ivar had put some lead in one side of it, that might make it tip to one side. We ran our hands over every inch of the inside, but we've found nothing.

'Let's go to his shop,' said Finn, this morning. 'I can ask him if he has any work for me. You look around while I keep him talking.'

⌘

I did find something yesterday! Amongst the small, sharp knives there was one knife with a black smudge of pitch on its tip. Why would a shoemaker use pitch? Father does, though — not on the insides of boats, but on the outsides.

⌘

We found it last night! A great lump of lead had been poured into one of the seams where the strakes are joined to each other. This morning we told Father what we found.

Did you know?

The water of Dublin Bay used to come right up to Pearse Street, at the back of Trinity College. People who lived on Pearse Street had the right to catch fish from their windows.

2000 2000 2000 2000 2000 2000 2000 2000 2000 2000 2000 2000 2000

2000 2000 2000 2000 2000 2000 2000 2000 2000 2000 2000 2000 2000

2000 2000 2000 2000 2000 2000 2000 2000 2000 2000 2000 2000 2000

2000 2000 2000 2000 2000 2000 2000 2000 2000 2000 2000 2000 2000

On 1 October 1795 the Royal College of St Patrick opened in Maynooth, County Kildare. It became a seminary for educating priests. It was known as St Patrick's College, Maynooth, but is now NUI Maynooth.

01

Sunday

* World Events

! My World

? Fact File

October October October October

02 Monday

2000 2000 2000 2000 2000 2000 2000 2000 2000 2000 2000 2000 2000

03 Tuesday

2000 2000 2000 2000 2000 2000 2000 2000 2000 2000 2000 2000 2000

04 Wednesday

2000 2000 2000 2000 2000 2000 2000 2000 2000 2000 2000 2000 2000

05 Thursday

2000 2000 2000 2000 2000 2000 2000 2000 2000 2000 2000 2000 2000

First Quar

06 Friday

2000 2000 2000 2000 2000 2000 2000 2000 2000 2000 2000 2000 2000

07

Saturday

08

Sunday

* World Events

! My World

? Fact File

October October October October

2000 2000 2000 2000 2000 2000 2000 2000 2000 2000 2000 2000 2000

2000 2000 2000 2000 2000 2000 2000 2000 2000 2000 2000 2000 2000

2000 2000 2000 2000 2000 2000 2000 2000 2000 2000 2000 2000 2000

2000 2000 2000 2000 2000 2000 2000 2000 2000 2000 2000 2000 2000

2000 2000 2000 2000 2000 2000 2000 2000 2000 2000 2000 2000 2000

On 2 October 1942, 338 people were lost off the coast of Donegal when a cruise ship called the *Curaçao* collided with the *Queen Mary* liner.

October

09 Monday
2000 2000 2000 2000 2000 2000 2000 2000 2000 2000 2000 2000 2000

Yom Kippur

10 Tuesday
2000 2000 2000 2000 2000 2000 2000 2000 2000 2000 2000 2000 2000

11 Wednesday
2000 2000 2000 2000 2000 2000 2000 2000 2000 2000 2000 2000 2000

12 Thursday
2000 2000 2000 2000 2000 2000 2000 2000 2000 2000 2000 2000 2000

13 Friday
2000 2000 2000 2000 2000 2000 2000 2000 2000 2000 2000 2000 2000

Full Moon

On 14 October 1882 Eamon de Valera was born in New York. His mother was from County Limerick and his father was Spanish. Eamon joined the fight for Irish freedom, and later became a politician and the third President of Ireland.

14 Saturday

15 Sunday

* World Events

! My World

? Fact File

October October October October

October

16 Monday
2000 2000 2000 2000 2000 2000 2000 2000 2000 2000 2000 2000 2000

17 Tuesday
2000 2000 2000 2000 2000 2000 2000 2000 2000 2000 2000 2000 2000

18 Wednesday
2000 2000 2000 2000 2000 2000 2000 2000 2000 2000 2000 2000 2000

19 Thursday
2000 2000 2000 2000 2000 2000 2000 2000 2000 2000 2000 2000 2000

20 Friday
2000 2000 2000 2000 2000 2000 2000 2000 2000 2000 2000 2000 2000

Last Quarter

2000 2000 2000 2000 2000 2000 2000 2000 2000 2000 2000 2000 2000

2000 2000 2000 2000 2000 2000 2000 2000 2000 2000 2000 2000 2000

2000 2000 2000 2000 2000 2000 2000 2000 2000 2000 2000 2000 2000

2000 2000 2000 2000 2000 2000 2000 2000 2000 2000 2000 2000 2000

2000 2000 2000 2000 2000 2000 2000 2000 2000 2000 2000 2000 2000

On 16 October 1890 Michael Collins was born in Clonakilty, County Cork. He became involved in the War of Independence. He was shot dead during the Civil War which followed the signing of the Treaty with Britain.

21 Saturday

22 Sunday

* World Events

! My World

? Fact File

October October October October

October

October

23 Monday

2000 2000 2000 2000 2000 2000 2000 2000 2000 2000 2000 2000 2000

24 Tuesday

2000 2000 2000 2000 2000 2000 2000 2000 2000 2000 2000 2000 2000

25 Wednesday

2000 2000 2000 2000 2000 2000 2000 2000 2000 2000 2000 2000 2000

26 Thursday

2000 2000 2000 2000 2000 2000 2000 2000 2000 2000 2000 2000 2000

27 Friday

2000 2000 2000 2000 2000 2000 2000 2000 2000 2000 2000 2000 2000

New Moon

2000 2000 2000 2000 2000 2000 2000 2000 2000 2000 2000 2000 2000

2000 2000 2000 2000 2000 2000 2000 2000 2000 2000 2000 2000 2000

2000 2000 2000 2000 2000 2000 2000 2000 2000 2000 2000 2000 2000

2000 2000 2000 2000 2000 2000 2000 2000 2000 2000 2000 2000 2000

2000 2000 2000 2000 2000 2000 2000 2000 2000 2000 2000 2000 2000

On 23 October 1641 the Ulster Rising began. It is believed that in the early days of the rebellion 12,000 Protestant men, women and children died.

30

Monday

2000 2000 2000 2000 2000 2000 2000 2000 2000 2000 2000 2000 2000

31

Tuesday

2000 2000 2000 2000 2000 2000 2000 2000 2000 2000 2000 2000 2000

Hallowe'en

*

World Events

2000 2000 2000 2000 2000 2000 2000 2000 2000 2000 2000 2000 2000

!

My World

2000 2000 2000 2000 2000 2000 2000 2000 2000 2000 2000 2000 2000

?

Fact File

2000 2000 2000 2000 2000 2000 2000 2000 2000 2000 2000 2000 2000

On 31 October 1867 William Parsons, the third Earl of Rosse, died. Between 1842 and 1845 he had had a huge telescope made in the grounds of Birr Castle in County Offaly. Until 1917, it was the biggest telescope in the world.

INVENTIONS

Many of the things we take for granted — electricity, cars, even things like sugar and glass windows — would have seemed incredible to someone living a thousand years ago. What do you think are the greatest inventions of the past millennium? What things do you hope will be invented in this millennium?

Art's Story

Yesterday was Samhain. My family celebrated my return with a visit to the assembly at the sacred halls of Tara. We saw the horse-races and the fairs and the markets. There was much dancing and singing and drinking of mead.

Five days ago my mother began to weave me new clothes. My time to leave my family, and to join the druids, is coming near.

❖

My new trousers are ready. They have been woven from two different colours of wool: red, dyed with the juice of the root of madder, and blue, dyed with the woad plant. The colours are in squares. My mother is very pleased with them and so am I. They fit well and tightly around my legs.

My linen shirt has been sewn, too. Tomorrow, using the finest and softest calf-skins, my mother will start on my leather tunic.

Finn's Story

In three more days it will be the day of the Thing. Neither Ita nor I have ever been to a Thing, but we know that it's a meeting where laws are made and judgements are given. It's held each year on the Thing-mote, the little hill on Hoggen Green, only a few minutes' walk from where we live.

⌘

Today Father told us that we'll have to speak at the Thing tomorrow and tell how we found the lead and how we saw the pitch on the shoemaker's knife. We're both so nervous that we don't think we'll be able to sleep.

⌘

It's all over. Ivar the shoemaker has to pay Father eight pieces of gold, and all the people know why our boats sank. Once again, Father is the best boat-builder in Dublin.

Today Father cut the lead out of the boat, mended the strakes and poured liquid pitch over the side. Tomorrow he will test it.

2000 2000 2000 2000 2000 2000 2000 2000 2000 2000 2000 2000 2000

Our World

The so-called Seven Wonders of the Ancient World are:

The Pyramids of Egypt

The Hanging Gardens of Babylon

The Statue of Zeus at Olympia

The Temple of Artemis at Ephesus

The Tomb of Mausolus at Halicarnassus

The Colossus of Rhodes

The Pharos of Alexandria

01
Wednesday

2000 2000 2000 2000 2000 2000 2000 2000 2000 2000 2000 2000 2000

02
Thursday

2000 2000 2000 2000 2000 2000 2000 2000 2000 2000 2000 2000 2000

03
Friday

2000 2000 2000 2000 2000 2000 2000 2000 2000 2000 2000 2000 2000

First Quarter

2000 2000 2000 2000 2000 2000 2000 2000 2000 2000 2000 2000 2000

2000 2000 2000 2000 2000 2000 2000 2000 2000 2000 2000 2000 2000

2000 2000 2000 2000 2000 2000 2000 2000 2000 2000 2000 2000 2000

2000 2000 2000 2000 2000 2000 2000 2000 2000 2000 2000 2000 2000

2000 2000 2000 2000 2000 2000 2000 2000 2000 2000 2000 2000 2000

On 1 November 1625 Oliver Plunkett was born in County Meath. He later became Archbishop of Armagh. He was hung, drawn and quartered in 1681. He was canonised in 1975, becoming the first Irish saint since Laurence O'Toole.

04
Saturday

05
Sunday

* World Events

! My World

? Fact File

November November November November November November

06 Monday

07 Tuesday

08 Wednesday

09 Thursday

10 Friday

2000 2000 2000 2000 2000 2000 2000 2000 2000 2000 2000 2000 2000

2000 2000 2000 2000 2000 2000 2000 2000 2000 2000 2000 2000 2000

2000 2000 2000 2000 2000 2000 2000 2000 2000 2000 2000 2000 2000

2000 2000 2000 2000 2000 2000 2000 2000 2000 2000 2000 2000 2000

2000 2000 2000 2000 2000 2000 2000 2000 2000 2000 2000 2000 2000

November

11

Saturday

12

Sunday

*

World Events

!

My World

?

Fact File

November November November November

Full Moon

2000 2000 2000 2000 2000 2000 2000 2000 2000 2000 2000 2000 2000

2000 2000 2000 2000 2000 2000 2000 2000 2000 2000 2000 2000 2000

2000 2000 2000 2000 2000 2000 2000 2000 2000 2000 2000 2000 2000

2000 2000 2000 2000 2000 2000 2000 2000 2000 2000 2000 2000 2000

2000 2000 2000 2000 2000 2000 2000 2000 2000 2000 2000 2000 2000

On 8 November 1847 Abraham 'Bram' Stoker was born in Dublin. He was later to write the famous vampire story *Dracula*, which is partly set in a lonely castle in Transylvania.

13

Monday

2000 2000 2000 2000 2000 2000 2000 2000 2000 2000 2000 2000 2000

14

Tuesday

2000 2000 2000 2000 2000 2000 2000 2000 2000 2000 2000 2000 2000

15

Wednesday

2000 2000 2000 2000 2000 2000 2000 2000 2000 2000 2000 2000 2000

16

Thursday

2000 2000 2000 2000 2000 2000 2000 2000 2000 2000 2000 2000 2000

17

Friday

2000 2000 2000 2000 2000 2000 2000 2000 2000 2000 2000 2000 2000

18
Saturday

19
Sunday

* World Events

! My World

? Fact File

Last Quarter

2000 2000 2000 2000 2000 2000 2000 2000 2000 2000 2000 2000 2000

2000 2000 2000 2000 2000 2000 2000 2000 2000 2000 2000 2000 2000

2000 2000 2000 2000 2000 2000 2000 2000 2000 2000 2000 2000 2000

2000 2000 2000 2000 2000 2000 2000 2000 2000 2000 2000 2000 2000

2000 2000 2000 2000 2000 2000 2000 2000 2000 2000 2000 2000 2000

On 19 November 1798 Irish rebel Theobald Wolfe Tone died in prison. He was 35 and had killed himself to avoid execution.

20 Monday

2000 2000 2000 2000 2000 2000 2000 2000 2000 2000 2000 2000 2000

21 Tuesday

2000 2000 2000 2000 2000 2000 2000 2000 2000 2000 2000 2000 2000

22 Wednesday

2000 2000 2000 2000 2000 2000 2000 2000 2000 2000 2000 2000 2000

23 Thursday

2000 2000 2000 2000 2000 2000 2000 2000 2000 2000 2000 2000 2000

24 Friday

2000 2000 2000 2000 2000 2000 2000 2000 2000 2000 2000 2000 2000

New Moon

2000 2000 2000 2000 2000 2000 2000 2000 2000 2000 2000 2000 2000

2000 2000 2000 2000 2000 2000 2000 2000 2000 2000 2000 2000 2000

2000 2000 2000 2000 2000 2000 2000 2000 2000 2000 2000 2000 2000

2000 2000 2000 2000 2000 2000 2000 2000 2000 2000 2000 2000 2000

2000 2000 2000 2000 2000 2000 2000 2000 2000 2000 2000 2000 2000

25

Saturday

26

Sunday

* World Events

! My World

? Fact File

On **26 November 1791** the first convicts sent from Ireland arrived in the penal colony of Botany Bay. Between 1791 and 1853, 40,000 Irish men and women were transported to penal colonies in Western Australia.

27

Monday

2000 2000 2000 2000 2000 2000 2000 2000 2000 2000 2000 2000 2000

28

Tuesday

2000 2000 2000 2000 2000 2000 2000 2000 2000 2000 2000 2000 2000

Ramadan
begins

29

Wednesday

2000 2000 2000 2000 2000 2000 2000 2000 2000 2000 2000 2000 2000

30

Thursday

2000 2000 2000 2000 2000 2000 2000 2000 2000 2000 2000 2000 2000

2000 2000 2000 2000 2000 2000 2000 2000 2000 2000 2000 2000 2000

Did you know?
The old Saxon name for the month of November was Wind-monath (wind-month).
That was when the weather became so windy that the fishermen would bring their
boats ashore and stop fishing until the following spring.

Did you know?

The Irish language was brought to Ireland by Celtic invaders about three thousand years ago. Until the end of the eighteenth century, it was the language spoken by most people in Ireland, especially outside the cities. Some English words which are still used today come from old Irish words or phrases:

banshee — bean sídhe (fairy woman)
galore — go leor (plenty)
leprechaun — luchorpán (small-bodied creature)
Tory — tóraí (a hunter or outlaw)
whiskey — uisce beatha (the water of life!)

2000 2000 2000 2000 2000 2000 2000 2000 2000 2000 2000 2000 2000

2000 2000 2000 2000 2000 2000 2000 2000 2000 2000 2000 2000 2000

2000 2000 2000 2000 2000 2000 2000 2000 2000 2000 2000 2000 2000

On 30 November 1667 Jonathan Swift was born in Dublin. He became Dean of St Patrick's Cathedral and was the author of *Gulliver's Travels*.

EUROPEAN UNION

There are fifteen countries in the European Union. Ireland is one of them.
Below is a table of information about these countries.

Country	Capital	Population	Language	Currency
Austria	Vienna	8,132,000	German	schilling
Belgium	Brussels	10,615,000	Flemish/French	Belgian franc
Denmark	Copenhagen	5,305,000	Danish	Danish krone
Finland	Helsinki	5,137,000	Finnish	markka
France	Paris	58,609,000	French	French franc
Germany	Berlin	82,072,000	German	Deutschmark
Greece	Athens	10,616,000	Greek	drachma
Ireland	Dublin	3,607,000	Irish/English	punt
Italy	Rome	56,830,000	Italian	lira
Luxembourg	Luxembourg	420,400	French/Letzeburgish	Lux. franc
Netherlands	Amsterdam	15,650,000	Dutch	guilder
Portugal	Lisbon	9,238,900	Portuguese	escudo
Spain	Madrid	39,108,000	Spanish/Catalan	peseta
Sweden	Stockholm	8,865,000	Swedish	Swedish krona
UK	London	57,592,000	English	pound (Sterling)

EUROPEAN UNION

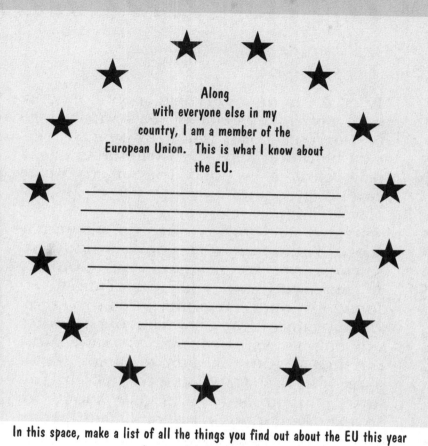

Along with everyone else in my country, I am a member of the European Union. This is what I know about the EU.

_____

_____

_____

_____

_____

_____

_____

_____

_____

In this space, make a list of all the things you find out about the EU this year that you didn't know before.

_____

_____

_____

_____

_____

_____

_____

_____

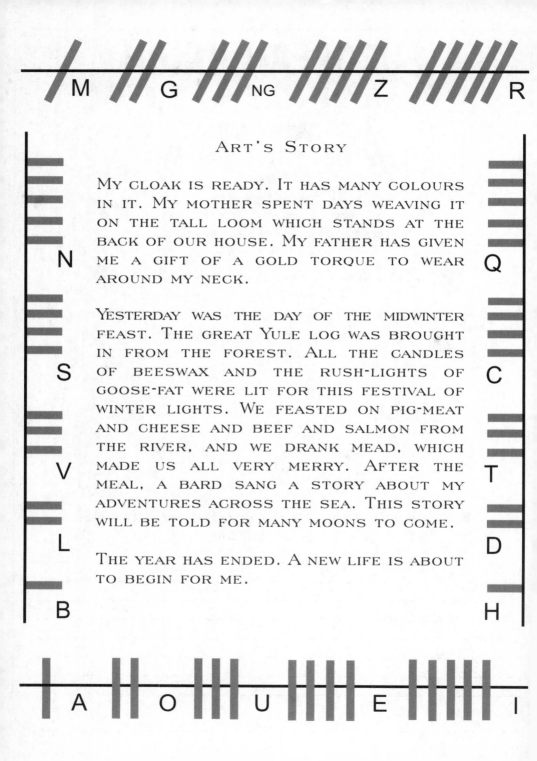

Art's Story

My cloak is ready. It has many colours in it. My mother spent days weaving it on the tall loom which stands at the back of our house. My father has given me a gift of a gold torque to wear around my neck.

Yesterday was the day of the midwinter feast. The great Yule log was brought in from the forest. All the candles of beeswax and the rush-lights of goose-fat were lit for this festival of winter lights. We feasted on pig-meat and cheese and beef and salmon from the river, and we drank mead, which made us all very merry. After the meal, a bard sang a story about my adventures across the sea. This story will be told for many moons to come.

The year has ended. A new life is about to begin for me.

Ita's Story

The boat sailed splendidly. Many people came out of their houses and down the street, to the quay at the side of the dark pool. They cheered when they saw the boat move out to the river.

⌘

Father has sold the new boat. Now we have money for everything. Today Finn got some new clothes: hose, a leather jerkin and a linen tunic. He looks very fine. I have a new gown, dyed a bright blue with woad. Over it I wear an apron, dyed yellow with onionskins and fastened at the shoulders with two brooches.

⌘

We've just had the best Christmas of our whole lives. We feasted on roast swan and salted herrings and cakes and ale, and even some Irish mead made from honey.

This is the last page of our yearbook. Soon Finn and I will go back to the monks to learn more. Maybe we'll make another yearbook sometime. I wonder if we'll ever have such a strange year again.

Now that you've seen the ancient Ogham writing that was used two thousand years ago, write a secret message in Ogham. Someday, when you re-read this yearbook, you'll be able to decode it.

2000 2000 2000 2000 2000 2000 2000 2000 2000 2000 2000 2000 2000

2000 2000 2000 2000 2000 2000 2000 2000 2000 2000 2000 2000 2000

2000 2000 2000 2000 2000 2000 2000 2000 2000 2000 2000 2000 2000

2000 2000 2000 2000 2000 2000 2000 2000 2000 2000 2000 2000 2000

2000 2000 2000 2000 2000 2000 2000 2000 2000 2000 2000 2000 2000

On 3 December 1976 Dr Patrick Hillery was installed as the sixth President of Ireland. On the same date in 1990 Mary Robinson became the seventh President of Ireland.

02
Saturday

03
Sunday

*

World Events

!

My World

?

Fact File

04

Monday

2000 2000 2000 2000 2000 2000 2000 2000 2000 2000 2000 2000 2000

First Quarter

05

Tuesday

2000 2000 2000 2000 2000 2000 2000 2000 2000 2000 2000 2000 2000

06

Wednesday

2000 2000 2000 2000 2000 2000 2000 2000 2000 2000 2000 2000 2000

07

Thursday

2000 2000 2000 2000 2000 2000 2000 2000 2000 2000 2000 2000 2000

08

Friday

2000 2000 2000 2000 2000 2000 2000 2000 2000 2000 2000 2000 2000

09

Saturday

10

Sunday

*

World Events

!

My World

?

Fact File

2000 2000 2000 2000 2000 2000 2000 2000 2000 2000 2000 2000 2000

2000 2000 2000 2000 2000 2000 2000 2000 2000 2000 2000 2000 2000

2000 2000 2000 2000 2000 2000 2000 2000 2000 2000 2000 2000 2000

2000 2000 2000 2000 2000 2000 2000 2000 2000 2000 2000 2000 2000

2000 2000 2000 2000 2000 2000 2000 2000 2000 2000 2000 2000 2000

On 6 December 1921 the Anglo-Irish Treaty was signed in London. Twenty-six of Ireland's thirty-two counties became the Irish Free State, while the remaining six Ulster counties remained a part of the United Kingdom.

11 Monday

2000 2000 2000 2000 2000 2000 2000 2000 2000 2000 2000 2000 2000

Full Moon

12 Tuesday

2000 2000 2000 2000 2000 2000 2000 2000 2000 2000 2000 2000 2000

13 Wednesday

2000 2000 2000 2000 2000 2000 2000 2000 2000 2000 2000 2000 2000

14 Thursday

2000 2000 2000 2000 2000 2000 2000 2000 2000 2000 2000 2000 2000

15 Friday

2000 2000 2000 2000 2000 2000 2000 2000 2000 2000 2000 2000 2000

2000 2000 2000 2000 2000 2000 2000 2000 2000 2000 2000 2000 2000

2000 2000 2000 2000 2000 2000 2000 2000 2000 2000 2000 2000 2000

2000 2000 2000 2000 2000 2000 2000 2000 2000 2000 2000 2000 2000

2000 2000 2000 2000 2000 2000 2000 2000 2000 2000 2000 2000 2000

2000 2000 2000 2000 2000 2000 2000 2000 2000 2000 2000 2000 2000

On 17 December 1834 Ireland's first railway was opened. It ran from Dublin to Kingstown. Kingstown is the old name for Dún Laoghaire.

December December December December December

16 Saturday

17 Sunday

* World Events

! My World

? Fact File

December

18 Monday

2000 2000 2000 2000 2000 2000 2000 2000 2000 2000 2000 2000 2000

Last Quarter

19 Tuesday

2000 2000 2000 2000 2000 2000 2000 2000 2000 2000 2000 2000 2000

20 Wednesday

2000 2000 2000 2000 2000 2000 2000 2000 2000 2000 2000 2000 2000

21 Thursday

2000 2000 2000 2000 2000 2000 2000 2000 2000 2000 2000 2000 2000

22 Friday

2000 2000 2000 2000 2000 2000 2000 2000 2000 2000 2000 2000 2000

23

2000 2000 2000 2000 2000 2000 2000 2000 2000 2000 2000 2000 2000

24

2000 2000 2000 2000 2000 2000 2000 2000 2000 2000 2000 2000 2000

*

World Events

2000 2000 2000 2000 2000 2000 2000 2000 2000 2000 2000 2000 2000

!

My World

2000 2000 2000 2000 2000 2000 2000 2000 2000 2000 2000 2000 2000

?

Fact File

2000 2000 2000 2000 2000 2000 2000 2000 2000 2000 2000 2000 2000

On 24 December 1601, at the Battle of Kinsale, the soldiers of Hugh O'Neill and Hugh O'Donnell were defeated by Lord Mountjoy's army.

25

Monday

2000 2000 2000 2000 2000 2000 2000 2000 2000 2000 2000 2000 2000

New Moon

Christmas Day

26

Tuesday

2000 2000 2000 2000 2000 2000 2000 2000 2000 2000 2000 2000 2000

St Stephen's Day

27

Wednesday

2000 2000 2000 2000 2000 2000 2000 2000 2000 2000 2000 2000 2000

28

Thursday

2000 2000 2000 2000 2000 2000 2000 2000 2000 2000 2000 2000 2000

29

Friday

2000 2000 2000 2000 2000 2000 2000 2000 2000 2000 2000 2000 2000

30 Saturday

31 Sunday

*

World Events

!

My World

?

Fact File

New Year's Day

2000 2000 2000 2000 2000 2000 2000 2000 2000 2000 2000 2000 2000

2000 2000 2000 2000 2000 2000 2000 2000 2000 2000 2000 2000 2000

2000 2000 2000 2000 2000 2000 2000 2000 2000 2000 2000 2000 2000

2000 2000 2000 2000 2000 2000 2000 2000 2000 2000 2000 2000 2000

2000 2000 2000 2000 2000 2000 2000 2000 2000 2000 2000 2000 2000

On 27 December 1904 the Abbey Theatre opened in Dublin. The first plays performed there were *On Baile's Strand* by W.B. Yeats and *Spreading the News* by Lady Gregory.

Me on
New Year's Eve
2000

My favourite memories of New Year's Eve 2000

My New Year's resolutions for the year 2001

(If you want to keep your resolutions extra-secret, why not tape a photo over them like a flap?)

January

01 Monday
2000 2000 2000 2000 2000 2000 2000 2000 2000 2000 2000 2000 2000

02 Tuesday
2000 2000 2000 2000 2000 2000 2000 2000 2000 2000 2000 2000 2000

03 Wednesday
2000 2000 2000 2000 2000 2000 2000 2000 2000 2000 2000 2000 2000

Holiday
UK and R
of Ireland

04 Thursday
2000 2000 2000 2000 2000 2000 2000 2000 2000 2000 2000 2000 2000

Holiday
Scotland

05 Friday
2000 2000 2000 2000 2000 2000 2000 2000 2000 2000 2000 2000 2000

J 2000

M		3	10	17	24	31
T		4	11	18	25
W		5	12	19	26
T		6	13	20	27
F		7	14	21	28
S	1	8	15	22	29
S	2	9	16	23	30

F 2000

M		7	14	21	28
T	1	8	15	22	29
W	2	9	16	23
T	3	10	17	24
F	4	11	18	25
S	5	12	19	26
S	6	13	20	27

M 2000

M		6	13	20	27
T		7	14	21	28
W	1	8	15	22	29
T	2	9	16	23	30
F	3	10	17	24	31
S	4	11	18	25
S	5	12	19	26

A 2000

M		3	10	17	24
T		4	11	18	25
W		5	12	19	26
T		6	13	20	27
F		7	14	21	28
S	1	8	15	22	29
S	2	9	16	23	30

M 2000

M	1	8	15	22	29
T	2	9	16	23	30
W	3	10	17	24	31
T	4	11	18	25
F	5	12	19	26
S	6	13	20	27
S	7	14	21	28

J 2000

M		5	12	19	26
T		6	13	20	27
W		7	14	21	28
T	1	8	15	22	29
F	2	9	16	23	30
S	3	10	17	24
S	4	11	18	25

J 2000

M		3	10	17	24	31
T		4	11	18	25
W		5	12	19	26
T		6	13	20	27
F		7	14	21	28
S	1	8	15	22	29
S	2	9	16	23	30

A 2000

M		7	14	21	28
T	1	8	15	22	29
W	2	9	16	23	30
T	3	10	17	24	31
F	4	11	18	25
S	5	12	19	26
S	6	13	20	27

S 2000

M		4	11	18	25
T		5	12	19	26
W		6	13	20	27
T		7	14	21	28
F	1	8	15	22	29
S	2	9	16	23	30
S	3	10	17	24

O 2000

M		2	9	16	23	30
T		3	10	17	24	31
W		4	11	18	25
T		5	12	19	26
F		6	13	20	27
S		7	14	21	28
S	1	8	15	22	29

N 2000

M		6	13	20	27
T		7	14	21	28
W	1	8	15	22	29
T	2	9	16	23	30
F	3	10	17	24
S	4	11	18	25
S	5	12	19	26

D 2000

M		4	11	18	25
T		5	12	19	26
W		6	13	20	27
T		7	14	21	28
F	1	8	15	22	29
S	2	9	16	23	30
S	3	10	17	24	31

Notes

Notes